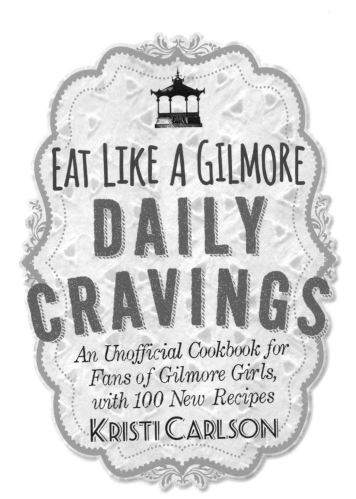

EAT LIKE A GILMORE
DAILY
CRAVINGS

An Unofficial Cookbook for
Fans of Gilmore Girls,
with 100 New Recipes

KRISTI CARLSON

Skyhorse Publishing

In memory of my brother, Ryan Carlson.

Skyhorse Publishing books may be purchased in bulk at special discounts for sales promotion, corporate gifts, fund-raising, or educational purposes. Special editions can also be created to specifications. For details, contact the Special Sales Department, Skyhorse Publishing, 307 West 36th Street, 11th Floor, New York, NY 10018 or info@skyhorsepublishing.com.

Skyhorse® and Skyhorse Publishing® are registered trademarks of Skyhorse Publishing, Inc.®, a Delaware corporation.

Visit our website at www.skyhorsepublishing.com.

10 9 8 7 6 5 4 3 2 1

Library of Congress Cataloging-in-Publication Data is available on file.

Cover design by Brian Anderson
Cover photos by Kristi Carlson
Photo of author by Tim David Kelly

Print ISBN: 978-1-51074-193-5
Ebook ISBN: 978-1-51074-194-2

Printed in China

EAT LIKE A GILMORE
DAILY CRAVINGS

CONTENTS

456

Author's Note

789

Kristi Carlson

To all of my fellow *Gilmore Girls* fans, I am very excited to introduce the new cookbook, *Eat Like A Gilmore: Daily Cravings*.

As you flip through these pages you may notice several of the themes, formats, and design elements from *Eat Like A Gilmore* have been carried over to this book. If you have the first book, this one will likely feel new, yet familiar, like a continuation. I guess that's what this book is—a continuation, yet still different and special in its own right.

Far more than the first book, this book digs into the eating habits of Lorelai and Rory. It highlights all the foods they craved on a daily basis—pizza, Chinese food, pie, ice cream, Pop-Tarts, and snacks from the many town festivals.

Making pizza and Chinese food at home is not something I ever had the urge to do. What first got me thinking about it was feedback from fans. So, to all the people who put that bug in my ear, thank you! Once I tried the first Chinese food recipe at home and it tasted just like take-out from a restaurant, but healthier, I was hooked. I also felt more like a Gilmore Girl than ever. Once you start making these recipes, my hope is you'll feel more like Lorelai or Rory, too.

While the recipes still directly tie in to the show, I put more emphasis on selecting recipes we can and want to use often in our daily lives, recipes we can add to our weekly meal rotation. In addition, I wanted to add recipes we can use to plan watch parties, dinner parties, and holiday dinners. Yes, this is a fan-based cookbook, but I hope you'll also find it to be a usable cookbook. Home cooks and folks who like to bake often have one or two cookbooks they use all the time, the ones with the worn covers and the splattered pages. That's what I set out to create here—a go-to cookbook we can rely on often, no matter the occasion.

The fundamentals are the same—butter is still butter, flour is still flour. These recipes have the same focus on whole ingredients as the recipes did in the first book. Some new townspeople have been added to the crew, so in addition to Luke's, Sookie's, and Emily's recipes, you'll also find recipes from Taylor's Soda Shoppe, Mrs. Kim's house, Al's Pancake World, and Weston's Bakery. The gang's all here!

After the fun and success we had with *Eat Like A Gilmore*, I would have understood if you all had said "one book is enough." Fortunately, you didn't. Through your Kickstarter pledges, your notes, and posts on social media you made it clear you want more.

Thanks to every single one of the 415 Kickstarter backers who funded this book, we now have more.

Thanks also go to the folks you'll meet in the coming pages, who contributed their recipes, their writing, their art, and their testing skills. They helped turn one fan's cookbook into a Gilmore family project.

In addition, I'd like to call attention to these wonderful people and say a public "thank you" to them:

Brian Anderson, the graphic designer who created every single beautiful page you see here, for showing up for this project in a big way, for all the late hours, long days, and touch-and-go moments, thank you.

Abigail Gehring, Tad Crawford, and Tony Lyons at Skyhorse Publishing for continuing to believe in this brand and in me.

Tony Escarcega and Gerome Huerta for generously offering vital help with cooking during the final weeks.

Ember Quillweb for lending her mad personal styling skills for the cover shot of me.

Khristina, Bryce, Sharon, Dawn, and the entire Cordova Crew for ongoing support and their endless willingness to taste test food.

Ian Harbilas for lending his time and skills to edit the video used in the Kickstarter campaign.

Jose Melgar and his team at Make Easy Maids for taking my kitchen from hopeless to spotless each week.

Finally, I'd like to thank my husband, **Tim Kelly,** for his patience, support, and hard work. During the writing of this book, he drove to the grocery store with me every morning and brought me lunch every afternoon. When I was photographing, he held the shade. When I needed music for the Kickstarter, he wrote and recorded it. When I forgot to buy an ingredient, he went and got it. When I needed to photograph "Luke," he put on a flannel shirt. Tim is the absolute best, and I'm so grateful to have had him with me throughout this process. This was our first major project as husband and wife – the first of many, I hope!

In the end, this book is for you, the fan. It is designed to keep Stars Hollow alive by making it feel a little closer, infusing a little bit of its essence into your homes. I hope it does that for you.

From my kitchen to yours,

Kristi

CONTRIBUTORS

Jennie Whitaker

Recipe Contributor:
Raspberry Peach Jam & Orange Marmalade

Location: Austin, Texas

First Episode Watched: S5/E3 "Written in the Stars"

When it comes to *Gilmore Girls*, Jennie has done just about everything except live in Stars Hollow. Alongside her husband, Marcus, she runs Seedling Communications in Austin. After an idea following the ATX TV Festival's "*Gilmore Girls* Reunion" in 2015, the two began screen printing *Gilmore Girls*-inspired tees under the shop name "Kindred Handicrafts." In the summer of 2016 she went on to plan the 1st *Gilmore Girls* Fan Fest, gathering fans from around the world in Connecticut each October. Let's just say that fateful day in 2009 really impacted her.

Visit Jennie's websites:
Gilmore Girls Fan Fest: **www.gilmoregirlsfanfest.com**
Kindred Handicrafts: **www.kindhandicrafts.com**
Seedling Communications: **www.seedling-communications.com**

Erica Summers

Writing Contributor: Homemade Pop-Tarts

Location: New York & Florida

Erica runs @GilmoreGirlsNews on Instagram and has an Etsy store where she combines her love of *Gilmore Girls* with her love of makeup, selling *Gilmore Girls*–themed merchandise, including candles, bath bombs, lip balms, and other beauty products. She also owns a beauty company called Summers Beauty Boutique.

Erica fell in love with *Gilmore Girls* from the pilot episode when it first aired in 2000. She was immediately hooked by the whole feel of the show, from the theme song, to the town, to the wonderful mother/daughter relationship between Lorelai & Rory. Stars Hollow always felt like home, and Lorelai & Rory felt like family.

Find Erica on Instagram at **@GilmoreGirlsNews**
Erica's Etsy store: **www.GilmoreThings.Etsy.com**
Erica's website: **www.summersbeautyboutique.com**

Natalie Schultz

Recipe Contributor: Strawberry Tarts

Location: Swansea, Illinois

Natalie's Haiku:

I bought this wrap dress
to look more like Lorelai.
We could be best friends.

Natalie Schultz is a middle school English and US history teacher, an aspiring author, and an independent consultant for the clean beauty brand Beautycounter. She believes that Stars Hollow can be brought to any "little corner of the world" with a dash of witty banter, a dollop of Sookie-style cooking, and a hefty helping of hometown love. Plus coffee—"in a vat." In her spare time, Natalie enjoys rewatching *Gilmore Girls* episodes, baking with her children, Evelyn, Cal, and Lorelei, and spending time with her husband, Zach.

Connect with Natalie:
www.beautycounter.com/natalieschultz
Instagram: **@beauty_clean_and_simple**
Email: **natalieschultz4409@gmail.com**

Tony Escarcega

Recipe Contributor: Chicken Salad

Location: Burbank, California

Favorite Episode: S2/E10 "The Bracebridge Dinner"

In his spare time, you can find Tony at the horse races, driving to Tucson to visit his family, taking a quick trip to Vegas, running through the sprinklers with the neighbors, making posole for his coworkers (the secret is in the hominy), or polishing his vast collection of Christmas tree ornaments. Tony loves the New England Patriots, classic country music, the color orange, and old pickup trucks. He's also a University of Arizona alumnus . . . Bear Down! Tony's "Team Jess" all the way, and wouldn't mind dating him, himself.

Kellie Beard & John Allen

Recipe Contributor: Fiesta Burger

Location: Lynchburg, Virginia

Kellie and John currently reside in Lynchburg, Virginia, with their two dogs, Nella and Charlie.

They share a love for growing spicy peppers and incorporating them into various dishes. Kellie and John enjoy being creative with their peppers, which has led them to grow a variety of peppers plants that typically are not found in your average grocery store.

Kellie has been a *Gilmore Girl* fanatic for years now and, though John doesn't like to admit it, there's a part of him that enjoys the wittiness of the show, as well. Kellie and John were extremely grateful to be able to contribute their love for spice (and *Gilmore Girls*) to this cookbook.

Brian Anderson

Recipe Contributor: Osso Buco

Location: Tucson, Arizona

Brian Anderson is a freelance art director by day and a cooking enthusiast at night. He is also a bass player, a lyricist, and a crummy golfer. He has three rescue Chihuahuas. Yeah . . . three. He is longtime friends with Tim and Kristi. He and Tim started their first garage band together when they were 16. He worked with Kristi to design the first *Eat Like a Gilmore* book and this one, as well. He has some mad skills in the kitchen and was delighted when Kristi asked him to contribute a recipe!

Visit Brian's website:
www.andersondesignaz.com

Gerome Huerta

**Recipe Contributor:
Spaghetti & Wheatballs & Tuna Loaf**

Location: Los Angeles, California

Car enthusiast. Stray pet magnet. Insomniac. Part-time server. Voiceover hopeful. Pescatarian convert. Just some of the things that make up a good amateur cook!

Growing up, cuisine at Gerome's house was complicated. The best chicken and dumplings, spaghetti, pot roast, or cornbread stuffing you could ever have was often followed by fast food, frozen pizza, and whatever was in the fridge. Now, twenty years after relocating to Los Angeles, cooking is Gerome's therapy and a creative outlet.

When he's not chasing a dog, he's likely chasing the next best plant-based burger . . . or asleep.

Find Gerome on Instagram: **@iamgerome70**

Fallon Hansen

Writing Contributor: Lobster Puffs

Location: Tampa, Florida

A Jane of many trades. Writing is one of those trades. A mom to a wonderful child, whom she hopes shares some of Rory Gilmore's habits. Married to a man who does not resemble Luke, but she loves him anyway. Fallon identifies with Lorelai in her overwhelming love for her child, passion for life, need for independence—yet stability in close friends—love of food, obsession for coffee, and ability to grow from the mistakes she has made. Fallon finds reading, writing, watching *Gilmore Girls*, and good food all feed her soul.

Connect on Instagram: **@ordinarymom**

Deidra Long

Writing Contributor: Sweet & Sour Pork

Location: Ohio

Favorite Episode: S4/E15 "Scene in a Mall"

Avid baker, food lover, movie collector, Gilmore Girl at heart. Deidra's fascination with cooking and baking started shortly after meeting her husband in 2011. With his patient demeanor, his keen listening, and his positive teachings, Deidra went from microwaved ravioli and store-bought cookies to prime rib feasts and homemade cheesecakes.

Because of her love of this new food venture, she finally stepped out of her comfort zone, leaped off that "conveyor belt," and became a baker for an amazing company. She now understands the phrase "find a job you enjoy doing, and you will never have to work a day in your life."

Visit Deidra's website:
beingnormalisboring.net

Michelle Tremblay

Artwork Contributor: Chapters 7 & 10

Location: Boston, Massachusetts

Favorite Episode: S2/E16 "There's the Rub"

Michelle Tremblay is a *Gilmore Girls* enthusiast, self-described ice cream connoisseur, travel lover, aspiring culinary aficionado, and avid reader. She attends Union College in Schenectady, New York, where she studies computer science, digital art, and French. She plans to be a graphic designer and hopes to start her own company one day. She strives to follow the motto, "Live more, laugh more, eat more, talk more, Gilmore."

Find her on Instagram: **@michelle__tremblay**

Heather Burson

Recipe Contributor: Mudd Pie

Location: Traverse City, Michigan

Heather's Haiku:

Dark hidden depths of
Clinging chocolatey layers.
A fork or shovel?

The accidental entrepreneur, Heather stumbled into opening Third Coast Bakery in 2013 when she left a radio broadcasting career to bake healthy desserts instead. Third Coast Bakery is 100 percent gluten-free, dairy-free, soy-free, and vegan, suppling retailers around Northern Michigan, in addition to welcoming customers to their new storefront/coffee bar. Heather regularly channels her inner Sookie when developing new recipes, opting for pigtails as the optimum hairstyle for successful baking. Heather is ridiculously addicted to coffee, chocolate, Lake Michigan, and *GG* reruns on Netflix.

P.S. There is nothing healthy about this recipe. Sookie would be proud.

Learn more about her bakery and shop online:
www.thirdcoastbakedgoods.com

Follow her on Instagram: **@thirdcoastbakery**

Like and follow her on Facebook:
www.facebook.com/thirdcoastbakery

Jessica Allbee

Artwork Contributor: Chapters 3 and 9

Location: Hudson Valley, New York

Favorite Episode: S04/E22 "Raincoats and Recipes" (where Luke & Lorelai finally kiss!)

Jessica is a lover of the ocean, music, animals, forest wandering, books, cooking, art, making people laugh, her wild family and friends, and, of course, rewatching *Gilmore Girls*. Contributing to this book was a wonderful way to combine several of her passions. She is thankful for those who helped her get here.

Follow her writing account on Instagram **@writeowl**

Reach her via LinkedIn:
www.linkedin.com/in/jessica-allbee-5487972a

Julie Arrington

Artwork Contributor: Chapters 1 and 9

Location: Virginia Beach, Virginia

Favorite Episode: S3/E22 "Those Are Strings, Pinocchio"

Julie's famous for quoting *Gilmore Girls* episodes. She's got merch, been on the studio tour, hit up a pop-up Luke's Diner, and still watches episodes weekly. She knew her husband was her "Luke" when he understood her Gilmore-isms (thanks to his daughter, Paige). Mutual *Gilmore Girls* love was how the trio bonded, and the fast-talking, quirky characters of Stars Hollow will always hold a special place in their little corner of the world.

Find Julie on Instagram: **@juliearrington15**

Lisa G. Larson

Writing Contributor: Marzipan

Location: Southern Utah

As a fellow fast-talking, junk food–loving, journalist-turned-writer and mom, Lisa G. Larson has loads in common with Lorelai and Rory, down to the special bonding that can only take place over family dinners. In real life Lisa loves attending the theater, enjoying the outdoors, reading, binge-watching her favorite TV shows, and spending time with her husband and three children. Her favorite foods include pasta, caramel popcorn, and anything combining chocolate and peanut butter.

Website: **www.lisaglarson.com**
Instagram: **@SoUtahScene**
Twitter: **@LisaGLarson**

Annemarie Conte

Recipe Contributor: Boston Cream Pie

Location: New Jersey

Annemarie's Haiku:

I was Team Logan
Then I did a full rewatch
Maybe Team Jess now?

Annemarie Conte is a magazine editor with an awesome husband and two adorable daughters. She bakes to de-stress, so she bakes *a lot*. She jumped at the chance to develop this Boston Cream Pie, which is actually a cake. And it's also her favorite flavor of donut. So that means it's a pie that's actually a cake that's actually a donut— which feels so very *Gilmore Girls*, doesn't it?

When she's feeling sad, she watches the "Michele has ennui" scene from "Love, Daisies and Troubadours," and it makes her laugh until she's not sad anymore. You should do that too.

Find her at **annemarieconte.com** and on Instagram **@annemarieconte**

Jessica Wheeler

**Writing Contributor & Recipe Tester:
Passion Fruit Sorbet**

Location: Pittsburgh, Pennsylvania

First Episode Watched: "The Pilot"

Jessica Wheeler was born and raised in the suburbs of Pittsburgh, Pennsylvania. She was honored to represent the city as Teen Miss Pittsburgh 1996. More than twenty years later, Jessica is a working mother of two with a focus on creating delicious and nutritious meals for her busy family. Her love of nutritious ingredients began when she was a little girl on her tiptoes in her mother's and grandmothers' kitchens. Her passion for desserts and comfort food also began in those kitchens, and Jessica continues the family traditions with her children.

To learn more about Jessica visit: **www.jessnwheeler.com**

Arianna Tzounako

Recipe Contributor: Chocolate Praline Cookies

Location: Downtown Saint Petersburg

Most Watched Episode: S6/E13
"Friday Night's Alright for Fighting"

Arianna Tzounakos is a business professional in the downtown Saint Petersburg area. Her hobbies include having cook-offs with her fiancé, baking, and spending quality time with her fur baby. Much like any Greek, Arianna insists on feeding all her family, neighbors, and friends. And now, thanks to Kristi Carlson, Arianna has the opportunity to feed fellow *Gilmore Girl* fans, without having to do the dishes.

Arianna's main goal in life is to be Emily Gilmore.

You can reach her at:
www.facebook.com/arianna.tzounakos
or Instagram **@air_tzoogs**

RECIPE TESTERS

Katlyn Allenson & Teri Patzwald

Location: Central Florida

Favorite Episode: S8/E4 "A Year in the Life – Fall"

A mother/daughter baking duo back for the second book! What makes them such a good team? Teri, the mother, has every baking tool and ingredient under the sun, while Katlyn, the daughter, has a knack for adding a twist to every recipe—not to mention Teri keeps the kitchen clean and Katlyn calm when things go awry mid-recipe.

Find Katlyn on Instagram: **@kpatzy**

Devin Avellino

Location: Horsham, Pennsylvania

Favorite Episode: S4/E22 "But I'm a Gilmore"

A married mother of two amazing kids, Devin loves staying busy between work, grad school, and volunteering at her son's school. In her free time, she enjoys spending time with family, traveling, and of course watching *Gilmore Girls*. She was also lucky to find her own friend like Sookie in college. Now she loves trying her own new cake creations as she starts her dream.

Find Devin on Instagram: **@davellino1115**
To learn more about Pasteries: **@pasteriessweets**

Andrea Blatt

Location: Eleanor, West Virginia

Favorite Episode: S4/E22 "Raincoats and Recipes"

When not watching *Gilmore Girls* with her best girl pals, Andrea is working full-time in sales, spending time with her family, or baking something yummy. She also enjoys traveling with her husband. They even visited Connecticut last year for their tenth anniversary so she could truly feel like a *Gilmore Girl*!

Rebecca S. Broomall

Location: Bloomington, Indiana

Favorite Episode: S6/E13 "Friday Night's Alright for Fighting"

Rebecca baked her first cake from scratch at age 7 after reading one of her mom's cookbooks. She is a telephony engineer by day and a home baker/unpublished writer in her spare time. She has two sons and one daughter who are *GG* fans just like Mom. She enjoys sharing her Lorelai-like coffee addiction with her husband Jeff.

Lauren Cutrone

Location: New Jersey

Favorite Episode: S4/E7 "The Festival of Living Art"

Lauren Cutrone is a marketing coordinator at a small publishing firm as well as a freelance writer. In her spare time she enjoys reading, cross-stitch, watching *Jeopardy!*, and convincing her friends that she isn't actually a senior citizen.

Find Lauren on Instagram: **@laurencutrone**

Erin Damm

Location: Bolingbrook, Illinois

Favorite Episode: S5/E6 "Norman Mailer, I'm Pregnant!"

Erin is a librarian and avid bookworm. When not reading, her free time is often spent baking, knitting and performing other crafty endeavors, and playing board games. She also enjoys traveling and creating memories with her husband, family, and friends.

Find Erin on Instagram: **@erinedamm**

Gabi Faber

Location: Chicago, Illinois

Favorite Episode: S5/E7 "You Jump, I Jump, Jack"

Recovered coffee addict, Gabi Faber can regularly be found deep in the throes of an intense Netflix binge (often of *Gilmore Girls*). Other hobbies include traveling, falling down internet rabbit holes, and pretending to be a wine expert. While she has kicked her coffee habit, she will still take that shot of cynicism any day.

Find Gabi on Instagram: **@gabifaber94**

Hannah Faber

Location: Chicago, Illinois

Favorite Episode: S2/E22 "I Can't Get Started"

Hannah Faber is currently a college student at the University of Kansas where she is studying to work with young children. Rock Chalk! Her hobbies include listening to music, going for long drives, and binging whatever show her older sister tells her to next. Oy with the poodles, already!

Find Hannah on Instagram: **@bananagyrl**

Meghan Fatticci

Location: Denver, Colorado

Favorite Episode: S3/E9 "A Deep Fried Korean Thanksgiving"

Meghan is a wife to a stud muffin and mama to three little loves and one big pup. She loves coffee and cookie dough. She first started watching *GG* with her mom when it originally aired, and through college she would have her mom tape episodes on VHS and mail them to her in her dorm. My, how times have changed!

Jamie Francis

Location: Rathdrum, Idaho

Favorite Episode: S2/E10 "The Bracebridge Dinner"

Jamie is a wife and stay-at-home mom of a wonderful, rambunctious nine-year-old. She loves to cook, bake, play Fortnite, and do all things *Gilmore Girls*. Her favorite character is Kirk. The cooking styles she relates to most are Luke's and Sookie's. Jamie and her husband, Gary, run a small business out of their home. It includes *Gilmore Girl* signs and many other styles of woodwork.

Join their Facebook group at **www.facebook.com/groups/bearwoodtreasures**

To see all their *Gilmore Girl* items, check out their website: **www.bearwoodtreasures.com**

Liz Groff

Location: Central Pennsylvania

Favorite Episode: S5/E7 "You Jump, I Jump, Jack"

A caffeinated blend of sarcasm and sass, Liz Groff is fluent in *Gilmore Girls* quotes for all occasions. Her wrist tattoo of "In Omnia Paratus" (complete with umbrella) is a handy icebreaker, especially when she's too nervous to talk to Scott Patterson after one of his gigs.

Learn more about this wanna-be Life & Death Brigader on Instagram **@ironlion4ever**

Emilia Hald

Location: Washington State

Emilia has been baking since she was young, when she started in the kitchen with her grandmothers, aunts, and mother. Her love of food led to two food science degrees. Now she enjoys baking for her family and learning how to make new things.

Rebecca B. Hofstetter

Location: Manchester, New Hampshire

Favorite Episode: S3/E9 "A Deep-Fried Korean Thanksgiving"

Rebecca lives in a 100-year-old house with her husband who she married under a Stars Hollow-esque gazebo in their New England town. Her favorite holiday is Halloween and she loves all things autumnal. She works in digital marketing and loves to bake, read, write, and sit on her front porch. *Gilmore Girls* has been her favorite show since the pilot aired in 2000.

Website: **thedoughtydoughnut.com**

Instagram: **@bostonbb**

Heather Huff

Location: Houston, Texas

Favorite Episode: S2/E10 "The Bracebridge Dinner"

Heather loves *Gilmore Girls* for the characters, relationships, festivals, and events. She looks forward to hosting movie nights like Lorelai and Rory, using recipes from the cookbook. She works as a number cruncher by day and her hobbies include photography, travel, and reading.

To learn more about Heather, visit her website: **www.talesfromalife.com**

Shannon Huffman

Location: Mt. Morris, Michigan

Favorite Episode: S4/E21 "Last Week Fights, This Week Tights"*

Shannon is a wife and mother of two. She works at ULTA Beauty as a Retail Sales Manager. She also has two YouTube channels. One is all things beauty and the other is all about her love of *Gilmore Girls*.

Simply Shannon: **https://m.youtube.com/channel/UClDtpqsLLf9_sKKVf_g84Hw**

Coffee at Luke's: **https://m.youtube.com/channel/UClmyV1YF2zXojAaDM5-u4Og**

Watching Luke and Lorelai dance at the wedding always makes her heart skip a beat. She also loves everything about TJ.

Cathi Kennedy

Location: St. Charles, MO (St. Louis area)

Favorite Episode: S4/E21 "Last Week Fights, This Week Tights"

Cathi is married and has two kids, Taylor (26) and Alex (22). She works in marketing and enjoys reading, cooking, and traveling. Cathi and Taylor share the love of *GG* and like to think their relationship is similar to Rory and Lorelai. Being a tester for the next *GG* cookbook combines Cathi's love of cooking and *GG*.

Find Cathi on Instagram: **@ckennedy66**

Nicky Krieger-Loos

Location: Dudelange, Luxembourg/Europe

Favorite Episode: S7/E21 "Unto the Breach"

Born and raised in Luxembourg, Nicky went on to move around the world with her family. They have lived in the USA, Austria, Russia, China, and currently in Brazil. She discovered many new recipes on the road and loves to try them at home. Friends and family also enjoy her unique and fun birthday cake—which you can discover on her Instagram **@nicky_in_the_kitchen.**

Heather Mainz

Location: Hastings, MN

Favorite Episode: "I love them all!"

Heather is a coffee-obsessed mother of a toddler boy and loves to bake while binge-watching *Gilmore Girls.* She personally identifies with the girls' coffee addiction!

Heather loves the bond Lorelai and Rory share and hopes to have a similar relationship with her son when he grows up.

Find Heather on Instagram: **@hmainz**

Melissa McAndrews

Location: San Jose, CA

Melissa is a 911 dispatcher for a Bay Area fire department. In her spare time, she is a photographer. She loves the beach, baseball, country music, and of course *Gilmore Girls*! She has a hard time picking a favorite episode. Every time she has a *Gilmore Girls* marathon, her favorites change!

Website: **www.500px.com/mismca**

Find Melissa on Instagram: **@mis.mca**

Sarah Panizza

Favorite Episode: S5/E7 **"You Jump, I Jump, Jack"**

Sarah Panizza is an amateur baker and cake decorator who loves to spend her free time lost in a book or daydreaming about holiday and travel plans. She has cooked her way through most of the first *Eat Like a Gilmore* cookbook and can't wait to make her way through this one. Picking a favorite *Gilmore Girls* episode was never going to be easy, but in the end it had to be "You Jump, I Jump, Jack"; though "The Party's Over" is definitely up there as one of the best because it is the end of Dean, once again.

Find Sarah on Instagram: **@sarahpanizza**

Sarah Lea Phelps

Location: New Jersey

Favorite Episode: S5/E7 "You Jump, I Jump, Jack"

Sarah Lea is a veteran recipe tester. Since the last book, she and her husband have welcomed a daughter, Aurora (Rory), who is undoubtedly her harshest culinary critic to date. Luckily, she looks to have inherited Mom's penchant for macaroni and cheese, and after they carbo-load they like to play outside. Where Aurora leads, Mom will always follow.

Find Sarah Lea on Instagram: **@sarahlea13**

Alyssa Race

Location: Upstate New York

Favorite Episode: S4/E2 "The Lorelais' First Day at Yale"

Alyssa Race is a wife, nurse, and dog mom who enjoys eating food, baking food, and running marathons (in that order). On her days off she also loves to watch *Gilmore Girls* with her dog Cheeto Puff and, thanks to her outstanding husband's appetite, she is a very practiced recipe tester.

Ashley Scarborough

Location: Elkville, Illinois

Favorite Episode: S7/E4 "'S Wonderful, 'S Marvelous"

Ashley loves anything to do with baking, from cookies to homemade pizza. Her hobbies include teaching American Sign Language to the people in her life, hiking, and spending time with her family and her bloodhound, Daisy May.

Lynn Tomei

Location: California

Nurse, travel wannabe, and new experience seeker, within reason. Taurus. Wife to a wonderfully amazing man and mom to boys with true hearts. A woman of the '80s who has finally learned to slow down and appreciate the simple pleasures this life has to offer.

"If I could only have one food to eat for the rest of my life? That's easy. Pez. Cherry Flavored Pez. No question about it."—Vern; *Stand by Me*

REFERENCE GUIDE

Abbreviations

t = teaspoon

T = tablespoon

c = cup

lb = pound

Ingredients

Butter = salted butter

Sugar = white, granulated sugar

Flour = all-purpose flour

Milk = whole milk

Vanilla = pure vanilla extract

Basic Equipment

Ninety percent of the recipes in this book can be made using this list of equipment.

If you're just beginning to equip your kitchen, investing in the items on this list will enable you to cook nearly everything—not just in this book, but in most any cookbook.

If you're on a budget, many of these items can be found very inexpensively at thrift stores and garage sales.

Dutch oven

Saucepan

Frying pan

Oven

Electric mixer

Blender and/or food processor

Coffee maker

9 x 14 baking pan

8 x 8 baking pan

Cookie sheet

Standard 8-inch pie plate

Large muffin pan

Candy thermometer

Meat thermometer

Heat-resistant rubber spatula

Slotted spoon

Wire whisk

Sharp chef's knife

Sharp serrated knife

Vegetable peeler

Grater

Strainer

Tongs

Pitcher

Measuring cups—dry ingredients

2-cup measuring cup—liquids

Measuring spoons

Cooling rack(s)

Piping bag

Drink shaker

Jigger

Muddler

Citrus squeezer or juicer

Ice cream maker

Dough cutter

Pastry cutter

Tart pans

Springform pan

Tarts, Pastries & Jams

HOMEMADE POP-TARTS®

If coffee is the soul of Gilmore girls, then Pop-Tarts are their hearts. Pop-Tarts are one of the most iconic foods in Gilmore world, and we're very excited to include this recipe in the second *Eat Like a Gilmore* cookbook. These Homemade Pop-Tarts are so yummy, they may redefine your entire existence, just like they did for Lorelai. The very first time she tasted a Pop-Tart it changed her whole outlook on life and inspired her to be the Lorelai Gilmore we all know and love. And if you find yourself in need of a pregnancy test, throw some Pop-Tarts on a plate with an apple in the middle and see which one you crave. If it is the apple, you may have your very own Rory in the oven. But if a Pop-Tart calls to you, it's just a normal day in the life of a Gilmore Girl.

For crust:

2 T	Butter
1 c	Flour
2 T	Almond meal
¼ t	Baking soda
¼ t	Salt
1 T	Coconut oil
1 T	Corn syrup, light
1 T	Sugar
1	Egg
1 T	Milk

For brown sugar cinnamon filling:

¼ c	Brown sugar
1 T	Sugar
½ t	Cinnamon
1 T	Corn syrup, dark
½ t	Molasses

For maple icing:

1 c	Powdered sugar
2 T	Corn syrup, dark
1 T	Maple syrup, pure
1 T	Milk

For lemon filling:

¼ c	Sugar
1 T	Corn syrup, light
1 T	Lemon juice, freshly squeezed
	Zest of one lemon

For lemon icing:

1 c	Powdered sugar
1 T	Corn syrup, light
1 t	Lemon juice, freshly squeezed
	Zest from 2 lemons

For strawberry filling:

¼ c	Sugar
1 T	Corn syrup, light
1 T	Strawberry jam, strained to remove liquid
1 t	Strawberry extract

For strawberry icing:

1 c	Powdered sugar
1 T	Corn syrup, light
1 t	Strawberry extract
1 T	Milk

Prepare pan and oven: Set out a baking sheet and cover with parchment paper or a silicone mat. Set aside. Ensure oven rack is in center position. Preheat oven to 350°F.

Brown butter: Place butter in small saucepan over medium heat. Once butter melts, let it continue to cook until it turns a medium caramel brown. Butter will foam. Once the foam begins to disappear, the butter will be the correct color. Remove from heat.

Mix dry ingredients: In a medium bowl, combine flour, almond meal, baking soda, and salt. Set aside.

Mix wet ingredients: In a large bowl, combine coconut oil with 2 tablespoons brown butter. Add corn syrup and sugar; stir with fork to combine. Whisk in egg, then milk.

Make dough: With a large fork or wooden spoon, mix dry ingredients into wet ingredients until fully combined and dough is smooth.

Roll out dough: Lightly flour a flat work surface. Lay dough in center of surface. Sprinkle top of dough with light layer of flour. With a rolling pin, roll dough into a large rectangle until it is very thin—about 1/16th of an inch. Use a cutter in the shape you'd like. To make a traditional rectangular tart, use a knife to cut it out, or the bottom of a box grater may work. Place the cutouts onto the prepared pan. Set aside.

Make filling: In a medium bowl, combine all ingredients and mix with fork until fully combined. Spoon 1 tablespoon of filling onto each cutout piece of dough on pan. Gently spread filling

Continued on the next page . . .

Intro by Erica Summers

Eat Like a Gilmore DAILY CRAVINGS

so it covers as much of the dough as possible, avoiding the outer ¼ inch border.

Prepare tarts: Place the remaining cutouts of dough on top of the tarts already on the pan. Line up the top crust with the bottom crust, then use your fingers to press the edges together. To get a very finished look, use a dough cutter or pizza cutter to trim a tiny bit of the edge off, all the way around each tart. Discard trimmings.

Bake tarts: Place pan in oven for 6 minutes. Remove from oven promptly. Let cool.

Make icing: In a medium bowl, combine all ingredients. Mix together with a fork until icing reaches a smooth, creamy consistency.

Ice tarts: Use a teaspoon to spoon icing onto a cooled tart. Use the back of the spoon to spread the icing, covering the top in a thin, even layer. Place tart on a plate to set. Repeat for remaining tarts. Serve.

s6 e3

Tester—Lauren Cutrone

STRAWBERRY TARTS
CONTRIBUTED BY NATALIE SCHULTZ

SOOKIE'S KITCHEN

Did you ever wonder if Lorelai could be a great cook if she just tried? Or think maybe the fact that she rarely does anything culinary is mostly due to her lack of interest in baking rather than any lack of skill? Generally speaking, Lorelai is a wonderfully talented woman—she runs the inns with style and ease, she is a terrific mother to Rory, she loves to paint diners, she writes eloquent character references. She even created her own version of a she-shed in her garage after the boat was gone. So, could Lorelai be a great cook and baker, if she only tried?

Nothing screams "NO!" to this question quite like Sookie's story about the strawberry tarts. Baking with girlfriends is fun, so it's understandable Sookie would try to teach Lorelai to bake something so the two of them could share a fun time in the kitchen. Cut to Sookie having to repaint the kitchen wall red after Lorelai exploded strawberry juice everywhere. Lesson learned (by Sookie, not Lorelai)!

These little tarts can make a mess. Not a paint-the-wall-when-you're-done mess, mind you. Still, when you taste those sweet berries tucked into their light crust, any bit of mess will be worth it.

For dough:

½ c	Butter, softened
½ c	Sour cream, room temperature
1¼ c	Flour
	Additional butter, shortening, or nonstick spray

For filling:

7–8 c	Strawberries, fresh, washed, stemmed, *divided*
¾ c	Sugar
3 T	Lemon juice, freshly squeezed
1 c	Cold water
3 T	Cornstarch

For topping:

2 c	Heavy cream
½ c	Superfine sugar
1 t	Vanilla extract
¼ c	Sour cream

Prepare pans and oven: Set 8 5-inch tart pans or ramekins on a baking sheet. Grease the bottoms with butter, shortening, or nonstick spray. Set aside. Ensure the oven rack is in the center position. Preheat oven to 375°F.

Make dough: In a medium bowl, using an electric mixer, cream butter and sour cream. Add flour gradually. Continue beating with mixer until a dough forms.

Press dough into pans: Measure ¼ cup of dough by pressing dough into a measuring cup. Transfer dough to one of the tart pans. Press dough into the pan, into all pleated edges, and flatten the area starting at the center of the dough up to ⅛ of an inch before the edges. This will create a slight "lip" around the crust to hold in the gelatin. Repeat for all dough.

Bake crusts: Place pan in oven. Bake for 20 minutes. Some crusts may still look light, with no browning around edges; others may show slight browning. Both are fine. Remove pan from oven and let cool for 10 minutes. Transfer tart pans to a cooling rack for crusts to cool completely.

Prepare strawberries: Select 32–35 of the prettiest, most evenly sized, 1–1½-inch berries. Slice them into ¼-inch slices, from top to bottom of berry. Arrange the berry slices in the tart pans, roughly 16 slices per tart, in the desired pattern. Set aside.

Cook strawberries: Place the remaining berries in a medium saucepan. Add sugar and lemon juice. Cook the berries over medium heat, stirring and mashing strawberries as they cook, for 10 minutes. This step will extract the water and sugar from the berries. Remove pan from heat. Strain berries, collecting all liquids in a bowl. You'll need 1 cup of liquid. If you are just shy of the full cup, press the solids in the strainer to extract all remaining liquids. Discard solids. Return 1 cup of liquid/syrup to the saucepan.

Thicken syrup: In a measuring cup, combine water and cornstarch. Stir to mix, until cornstarch is fully dissolved. Stir into strawberry syrup. The color will be a vibrant hot pink. Over medium-high heat, bring strawberry syrup to a boil, stirring constantly. When the color deepens to a darker magenta, that's the cue it's getting closer to boiling. Once boiling begins, you will also feel it thickening. Continue to heat and stir until mixture has fully thickened—about 30 seconds after boiling begins. Remove from heat. Continue to stir for 1–2 minutes to release heat.

Make tarts: Let thickened syrup cool to room temperature, but no longer. Pour 3–4 tablespoons of liquid into each tart pan until all strawberries have been at least partially covered. Refrigerate tart pans for 45 minutes.

Make whipped cream topping: In a large mixing bowl, combine heavy cream, sugar, and vanilla extract. With mixer set on medium speed, beat until stiff peaks form. Gently fold in sour cream. Beat on high again until stiff peaks form. Cover bowl with lid or plastic wrap. Chill until ready to serve tarts.

Serve tarts: Remove tarts from refrigerator. Remove tarts from pans (or serve them in their pans). Top each with a dollop of whipped cream topping. Serve.

s1 e12

FRUIT TART

She must have cooked and baked for days leading up to the basket-bidding event, all to surprise Jackson. At the time, they were still dating, so Sookie, understandably, wanted to make the basket extra special. One of the dishes she made is this fruit tart. We see it sitting on her silver table, looking gorgeous, right as Jackson walks in and nearly ruins the surprise!

Follow Sookie's example—this tart is a delicious way to say "I love you" to the person who cares about you so much, they'd even bid on your basket.

For pastry cream:

2 T	Butter
1 t	Vanilla extract
2 c	Heavy cream
3	Egg yolks
4 T	Cornstarch
⅓ c	Sugar
Pinch	Salt

For crust:

½ c	Butter, softened
½ c	Sugar
1 t	Vanilla extract
1 T	Heavy cream
1¼ c	Flour

For fruit topping:

15–20	Strawberries
15–20	Seedless grapes
20–30	Raspberries
20–30	Blueberries
3–4	Kiwi
	Peaches, *optional*

Prepare butter and vanilla: In small bowls or ramekins, measure and set aside butter and vanilla, so they are ready to go and easy to access when needed.

Prepare pastry cream: In a large saucepan, bring cream to a simmer over medium heat. While cream is warming, quickly whisk the yolks in a large mixing bowl. Add cornstarch; whisk to combine. Add sugar and salt; whisk again until fully combined. Once cream begins to simmer, remove from heat.

Temper eggs: While quickly whisking the egg yolk mixture, pour in 1 tablespoon of the cream. Continue to whisk and add 2 tablespoons of cream. Gradually add more and more cream while continuing to whisk quickly, until all cream has been incorporated.

Thicken pastry cream: Return mixture to saucepan and bring to a simmer over medium-high heat. Once the cream begins to thicken and bubbles are forming rapidly around the edges of the pan, remove from heat. Add butter and vanilla and whisk quickly to combine. Continue to whisk until custard cools a bit. Pour into a heat/cold-proof bowl. Cover with plastic wrap placed directly onto the top of the custard. Refrigerate 4 hours.

Prepare pans and oven: Set out an 8½-inch tart pan. Ensure oven rack is positioned in the center of oven. Preheat oven to 350°F.

Make crust: In medium mixing bowl, combine butter and sugar using a mixer. Add vanilla and heavy cream and mix to combine. Add flour. Mix until fully combined.

Bake crust: Scoop dough into tart pan and press so dough is flat and is inserted into every fold of tart pan. Place in oven and bake for 17–18 minutes. Crust will be very slightly browned in places. Remove from oven and let cool for 10 minutes. Remove from pan, place on plate, and let cool for 1 hour.

Prepare fruit: Wash and dry fruit. Remove stems, pits, and cores. Slice into desired shapes and sizes.

Assemble fruit tart: Scoop pastry cream onto crust and gently spread it to cover the entire surface, evenly. Place fruit on top of pastry cream in any design you'd like. Chill tart for 1 hour. Cut and serve.

s2 e13

Tester—Erin Damm

BROCCOLI TARTS

After the Inn closed, Sookie and Lorelai started a party-planning and catering business. Apart from hosting one children's birthday party, we didn't really see them get many gigs, until Emily Gilmore called. To prepare for the launch party, Sookie immediately started preparing lots of food. Lots of Broccoli Tarts. So many that Rory's room was filled with tray after tray of them. You may wonder—why would she make so many of these tarts for the party? How good can they be? It's broccoli. Once you've tried these, you'll know the answer. The layered savory flavors meld together so well. Plus, eating anything is more fun when it's in the form of a tart. Try one! Just don't call it a "quiche."

Crust:

1½ c	Flour
1 t	Salt
½ t	Sugar
½ c	Olive oil
3 T	Milk
1 T	Ice water

Filling:

2 T	Butter
⅔ c	Peeled and minced shallots
1½ c	Minced leeks
1 clove	Peeled and minced garlic
1 oz	White wine, dry
¼ t	Sugar
6 c	Chopped fresh broccoli
2 T	Half-and-half (or 1 T each of milk and cream)
1	Egg
½ t	Salt
¼ t	Pepper
1 c	Shredded aged white cheddar cheese, *divided*

Prep pans and oven: Set out mini tart pans with enough cups for 24 tarts. Ensure oven rack is positioned in center of oven. Preheat oven to 375° F.

Prepare dough for crust: In a medium mixing bowl, combine flour, salt, and sugar. Add oil and milk. Mix with a fork or pastry cutter until combined. Add ice water. Mix again until dough forms a large ball. If necessary, mold into a ball by hand. Place 2 teaspoons of dough into each tart cup. Press the dough into place so the bottom of each cup is fully covered, there is a "well" in the center of the dough, and the dough comes up the sides roughly a half inch. Repeat for 24 cups. Set aside.

Boil water: In a large saucepan or Dutch oven, bring 8–10 cups of water to a rolling boil.

Caramelize shallots, leeks, and garlic: While waiting for the water to boil, in a frying pan or Dutch oven, over medium-high heat, melt butter. Add shallots, leeks, and garlic. Cook until shallots and leeks are just beginning to brown along the edges. Add wine and combine. Sprinkle with sugar. Continue to cook until shallots and leeks turn medium brown. Remove from heat. Let cool for 10 minutes.

Blanch broccoli: Get out 2 large bowls and a slotted spoon. Fill one bowl halfway with cold/ice water. Once water in the pot is boiling, add broccoli pieces to the pot. Cook broccoli for 2 minutes only. Use the slotted spoon to remove broccoli from boiling water and place into the cold water. Once all broccoli is in the cold water, use slotted spoon to remove the broccoli from the cold water and place it in the empty bowl. Remove water from heat and discard. Also discard the cold water.

Make filling: Add half-and-half, egg, salt, and pepper to broccoli. Mix. Add shallot and leek mixture to broccoli. Mix. Add a half cup of grated cheese and mix. This is your filling.

Make tarts: Fill each tart cup with 1½–2 tablespoons of broccoli mixture. Top each tart with a pinch of grated cheese.

Bake and serve: Bake tarts for 15 minutes at 375° F. Remove from oven. Let cool for 5 minutes. Serve.

Tester—Emilia Hald

CINNAMON BUNS

Yale Days

Surely one of the things Logan loved most about Rory is the way she effortlessly moves back and forth from being the tiara-wearing debutante to the "I'll be the one in the bonnet" volunteer Pilgrim. Her high-society Gilmore background mixes with her down-to-earth Stars Hollow upbringing, giving her a uniquely well-rounded personality. Having Rory in his life gives Logan the opportunity to experience many normal-seeming things he never got to experience as a Huntzberger child—like birthday parties.

For Logan's 24th birthday, Rory is determined to make up for all the parties he missed. She organizes games, activities, and food so he can have that normal experience. She kicks it all off by bringing him warm cinnamon rolls in bed, which sounds like a terrific way to kick off a birthday . . . or any day!

For dough:

1½ c	Milk
1 pkg	Active dry yeast
½ c + 1 t	Sugar
4½ c	Flour (plus more for rolling dough)
1 t	Salt
6 T	Butter, room temperature
1	Egg, room temperature
1 t	Vanilla extract

For filling:

¼ c	Sugar
⅓ c	Brown sugar
¼ c	Cinnamon
6 T	Butter, melted
	Raisins, *optional*
	Chopped nuts, *optional*

For frosting:

4 T	Butter, room temperature
⅓ c	Cream cheese, room temperature
1½ c	Powdered sugar
2 t	Milk
1 t	Vanilla extract

Bloom yeast: In a medium saucepan, heat milk over medium heat until it reaches 100°F. Remove from heat. Sprinkle with yeast. Do not stir. Sprinkle with 1 teaspoon sugar. Do not stir. Let sit for 10 minutes. After 10 minutes the mixture should have bubbles and a light foam forming. (If there is no activity, the yeast is likely inactive. Discard mixture and start again.)

Make dough: In a medium mixing bowl combine flour and salt. Set aside. In a large mixing bowl, combine butter and ½ cup sugar using a mixer. Add egg and mix until fully combined. Add vanilla and mix. Alternate adding yeast mixture and flour/salt mixture until all ingredients have been incorporated and have formed a dough.

Let dough rise: Using butter, lightly grease the inside of a large mixing bowl. Set aside. Cover a flat work surface with a light layer of flour. Turn dough out onto surface and knead by hand for 20–25 turns. Form dough into a ball and place it into the greased bowl. Cover it with a kitchen towel and allow it to rise for 90 minutes.

Punch down dough: Once dough has doubled in size, gently press down the center of the dough all the way to the bottom of the bowl. Then carefully pull the edges of the dough away from the bowl and pull those edges toward the middle. Cover a flat work surface with a light layer of flour. Remove the dough from the bowl and place it on the flour. Knead dough for 5 turns. Let it rest for 10 minutes, covered with kitchen towel.

Make filling: In a medium mixing bowl, combine sugar, brown sugar, and cinnamon for the filling.

Make rolls: Cover a rolling pin with a light layer of flour. Use rolling pin to roll the dough into a large rectangle 18 inches wide by 12 inches tall. Brush dough with melted butter.

Generously sprinkle with cinnamon sugar mixture until dough is fully covered. Sprinkle with nuts and/or raisins, if using. Beginning at one end, fold dough over by 1 inch, then carefully roll the dough so it forms one large roll. Some parts of the dough may be stuck to the work surface. If so, use a dough cutter to scrape the dough loose as you go.

Cut rolls: Brush the bottom and sides of a 9x13-inch baking pan with the remaining melted butter. Using a sharp knife, cut the roll into 12 equal pieces. Place each piece swirl-side up in the baking pan. Once pan is full, cover with kitchen towel and allow to rise for 1 hour.

Make frosting: While rolls are rising, make the frosting. In a medium mixing bowl, combine butter and cream cheese using mixer. Sift in the powdered sugar. Mix to combine. Add remaining ingredients and mix until smooth. Set aside.

Bake rolls: Ensure oven rack is in center position. Preheat oven to 350°F. Place pan in oven and bake for 20–22 minutes. Remove from oven and let cool for 10 minutes. Brush tops with frosting and serve.

s7 e15

Tester—Erin Damm

Eat Like a Gilmore DAILY CRAVINGS

CHOCOLATE ÉCLAIRS

Christopher blew it at Parents' Weekend at Yale by inviting all of the *Daily News* team to join Rory, Lorelai, and him at lunch. Then, at lunch, he invited them all to a ski vacation, and he got everyone a little drunk. For many viewers this was a difficult scene to watch—the awkwardness was palpable.

After the lunch was over and the team was back to work in the newsroom, whose idea do you think it was to bring them all éclairs? Was it Christopher trying to right his wrong or Lorelai trying to fix the situation?

Whichever of them had the idea, it was a good one. They pair perfectly with coffee and they really do make work feel far less stressful.

For filling:

1 T	Butter
1 T	Vanilla
4	Egg yolks
1 c	Sugar
¼ t	Salt
2 c	Whole milk
4 T	Cornstarch
1 c	Heavy cream

For shells:

½ c	Butter, softened
1 c	Water
1 c	Flour
½ t	Salt
5	Eggs, *divided*

For glaze:

2 sq	Semisweet baking chocolate (may substitute 6 T semisweet chocolate chips)
2 T	Butter
1 c	Powdered sugar
1 T	Corn syrup
2–3 T	Milk

To make filling:

Prepare ingredients: Measure out butter and vanilla. Set aside (you'll need these in a hurry). In a medium mixing bowl, beat egg yolks. Add sugar and salt. Stir to combine. Set aside.

Heat milk: Add cornstarch to milk while milk is still cold. Stir until cornstarch is fully dissolved. In a large saucepan, bring milk to a simmer over medium heat. As soon as milk begins to simmer and tiny bubbles appear around the edge of the pan, remove from heat.

Temper eggs: While quickly whisking the egg yolk mixture, pour in 1 tablespoon of the hot milk. Continue to whisk and add 2 tablespoons of milk. Gradually add more and more milk while continuing to whisk quickly, until all milk has been incorporated. Whisk until smooth and fully combined.

Thicken custard: Pour mixture back into saucepan and bring to a simmer over medium heat, stirring often. As soon as custard begins to thicken and the first bubble reaches the surface, remove from heat, then add butter and vanilla. Stir until butter has fully melted. Continue stirring for about 2 minutes to keep custard smooth and release some of the heat.

Refrigerate: Pour into a bowl. Cover with plastic wrap, placed directly on top of the custard. Bring the custard to room temperature by keeping in on the counter, then refrigerate for 4 hours.

To make shells:

Prepare pan and oven: Cover a baking sheet with parchment paper. Set aside. Ensure oven rack is in center position. Preheat oven to 375°F.

Continued on the next page . . .

Tester—Heather Burson

Make dough: In a small saucepan, combine butter and water. Over medium heat, bring to a boil. Remove from heat. Add flour and salt. Use a wooden spoon or silicone spatula to combine. Dough will look lumpy. Return to medium-low heat. Cook the dough for a few seconds, until it smooths out. Use the wooden spoon/spatula to turn the dough several times in the pan as it cooks. Once dough is smooth and forms a ball, remove from heat.

Cool dough: Remove dough from pan and place in a medium mixing bowl. Allow the dough to cool for about a minute.

Make batter: In a small bowl, beat 4 of the eggs. Using an electric mixer, mix the dough on medium-low speed. Gradually add the beaten eggs to the dough. Once all eggs have been added, continue to mix until batter is smooth.

Bake shells: Scoop batter into a piping bag. Pipe dough onto the baking sheet in long, narrow lines, about 4 inches long. Leave 2–3 inches between each shell. Beat the remaining egg in a small bowl and brush the egg onto the tops of the shells. Place in oven and bake for 30–35 minutes. Shells should be golden brown on the top when done. Remove from oven. Let them cool completely.

To make glaze:

Melt chocolate: In a small saucepan, combine chocolate and butter. Melt the two together over medium heat. Once fully melted, remove from heat and let cool.

Mix glaze: In a medium bowl, combine powdered sugar, corn syrup, and 1 tablespoon of milk. Add chocolate mixture. Mix thoroughly. Add more milk as needed to get desired consistency.

To make éclairs:

Mix pastry cream: In a medium mixing bowl, whip cold heavy cream with an electric mixer until it forms peaks looking like thick ribbons. Fold cream into the cold custard. Mix thoroughly.

Assemble éclairs: Using a serrated knife, cut shells open, but not all the way through. Fold the shells open. Scoop pastry cream into a piping bag and pipe into shells. Apply glaze to top shells using a frosting knife, a butter knife, or the back of a teaspoon. Let glaze set slightly. Serve.

Makes 20–24 mini éclairs.

CHERRY DANISH

LUKE'S DINER

Watching *Gilmore Girls* teaches us a good cherry Danish goes with every life event. Just got divorced? Cherry Danish. Running into your ex all over town? Cherry Danish. Going through your deceased relative's papers? Cherry Danish. Works for everything.

For dough:

⅔ c	Milk
1 pkg	Active dry yeast
2 T + ½ t	Sugar
2¼ c	Flour
½ t	Salt
⅛ t	Cardamon
1	Egg
1 T	Butter, softened
1 c	Butter (2 sticks), cold

For cherry filling:

3 c	Cherries, fresh, stemmed and pitted
¾ c	Sugar
1 T	Lemon juice, freshly squeezed
2 T	Cornstarch

For Danish almond filling:

2 T	Almond meal
2 T	Powdered sugar
¼ t	Almond extract
5 T	Sugar
4 T	Butter
1	Egg
½ t	Vanilla extract
2 T	Flour

For glaze:

½ c	Powdered sugar
2 T	Water
2 t	Lemon juice, freshly squeezed

Bloom yeast: In a small saucepan, heat milk to 100–110°F. Remove from heat. Sprinkle yeast onto the milk. Then sprinkle ½ teaspoon of sugar on top. Let rest for 10 minutes. Watch for bubbling to occur and for a light foam to appear on top of the milk. These indicate the yeast is ready to use. (If no bubbling has occurred after 15 minutes, the yeast is likely ineffective. Discard the mixture and start again.)

Mix dough: In a large mixing bowl combine remaining sugar, flour, salt, cardamom, egg, and the 1 tablespoon of softened butter. Use an electric mixer on low speed to combine. Add the yeast mixture. Continue to mix on low to medium speeds until a dough forms.

Proof dough: Lightly oil or butter the inside of a large bowl. Scoop dough out of mixing bowl and into the greased bowl. Cover with a clean kitchen towel. Let dough rise for 1 hour. Next, punch down the dough—which sounds rough, but isn't. Gently push into the center of the dough until it is deflated. Then pull the edges away from the bowl and toward the center of the dough. Cover the bowl with plastic wrap and refrigerate dough for 2 hours.

Make butter layer: Cut cold butter into ¼-inch slices, lengthwise. On a piece of wax paper or plastic wrap, line them up, side by side. Sprinkle them with 2 teaspoons of flour, evenly. Then place another piece of wax paper or plastic wrap on top. Using a rolling pin, mash the butter slices together to form one square layer of butter about ¾-inch thick. Cut the butter layer in half. This butter should be cool, not melting. If you see signs of it melting, return it to the refrigerator for 10 minutes, then take it out and use it right away.

Continued on the next page . . .

Layer dough and butter: Remove the dough from refrigerator. Lightly flour a flat work surface. Using a rolling pin, roll out the dough into a wide rectangle, about 2 feet wide by 1 foot long. Place half the butter on the dough, in the center. (The long portion of the dough should be from left to right, while the long portion of the butter layer should be forward and back.) Fold one side of the dough over the butter.

Then place the second half of the butter layer on top of the dough you just folded over. Finally, fold over the other side of the dough. At this point you should have a smaller rectangle of dough with 5 layers: dough, butter, dough, butter, dough. Using your fingers, pinch all the openings closed.

1st fold: Rotate the dough one quarter turn so the widest part is stretching left to right in front of you. Use the rolling pin to roll the dough out to a 50 percent larger rectangle. Work in thirds again: fold the left third over the center third. Then fold the right third over the center third. Fold the whole thing in half. Then wrap the folded dough in plastic wrap and refrigerate for 15–20 minutes. (This step is to get the butter cold again.)

2nd fold: Remove dough from refrigerator. Lightly dust the work surface with flour, then roll dough out into another rectangle, same size as before. Fold it in thirds again, then fold the whole thing in half.

3rd fold: Repeat.

Refrigerate dough: Wrap dough in plastic wrap again and refrigerate a minimum of 2 hours, overnight recommended.

Masticate cherries: Place cherries into a large mixing bowl. Sprinkle evenly with sugar, lemon juice, and cornstarch. Mix gently to combine. Refrigerate a minimum of 3 hours, overnight recommended.

Make Danish almond filling: Place all ingredients into a medium bowl. Use an electric hand mixer to combine. Place filling in an airtight container and refrigerate until ready to use.

Later on, or next day:
Prepare pans: Cover 3–4 baking sheets with parchment paper or baking mats. Set aside.

Shape dough: Remove dough from refrigerator. Cut dough into thirds. Return two of the thirds to the refrigerator. Roll out the remaining third into a rectangle. Use a sharp knife or pizza cutter to cut the rectangle into six long strips. Working with one strip at a time, twist the strip several times, then arrange it on the pan in a spiral circle. Tuck the outside end under. Repeat for remaining strips. Once all strips have been shaped, cover pan with a clean dish towel and set aside. Repeat for the remaining two thirds of dough.

Prepare oven: Ensure oven racks are in central positions. Preheat oven to 375°F.

Assemble and bake: Press down the center each Danish to make a "cup" for the filling. Spoon 1 tablespoon of almond filling into cup. Then spoon cherries into cup. Bake for 15–20 minutes. Watch for Danish to turn golden brown. Remove from oven and let cool.

Glaze and serve: In a small bowl, combine the powdered sugar, water, and lemon juice until fully blended and smooth. Drizzle on fully cooled Danish. Serve.

FRUIT TURNOVERS

AT HOME

A Gilmore movie night always involves pizza and Pop-Tarts, often Chinese food, and tater tots seem to be a common favorite. To round out the menu, they also like to follow their food muse, throwing in one or two other foods they may be craving in the moment. By doing this, they make each movie night into its own unique little party.

One of the foods they added in is turnovers. Facing the dilemma of "cherry or apple," they arrived at the only logical answer—both!

This recipe uses premade dough. If you were in a big hurry, you could also use premade pie filling —so when you're looking to add some newness to your movie night repertoire, you can have these ready in a flash!

Apple Filling:

4 c	Peeled, cored, sliced apples, cut into ½-inch squares
½ c	Sugar
¼ c	Lemon juice, freshly squeezed
1 T	Cornstarch
2 T	Cold water
1 t	Cinnamon

Cherry Filling:

4 c	Cherries, stemmed and pitted
½ c	Sugar
¼ c	Lemon Juice, freshly squeezed
1 T	Cornstarch
2 T	Cold water
¼ t	Almond extract

Pastry:

4	Frozen premade puff pastry sheets (Pepperidge Farm recommended)
1	Egg
2 T	Water

Sweeten fruit: Choose either apple filling or cherry filling. Add the fresh fruit to a medium bowl. Sprinkle with sugar. Pour in lemon juice. Using a tablespoon or serving spoon, gently fold sugar and juice into fruit until combined. Let stand for 1 hour for apples, or 2–3 hours for cherries.

Thaw puff pastry: Remove puff pastry from freezer 30 minutes prior to assembling turnovers. Take care to use puff pastry within 40 minutes after removing it from the freezer.

Prep pan and oven: Place parchment paper or silicone mat on two cookie sheets. Set aside. Ensure oven rack is placed in the center of oven. Preheat oven to 400°F.

Strain fruit: Place a colander or fine mesh sieve over a medium saucepan. Pour in the fruit/sugar mixture. Drain the syrup from fruit into the pan. Gently shake the colander/sieve over the pan to strain as much of the syrup as possible. Once fully strained, return fruit to its bowl. Set aside.

Thicken syrup: In a small bowl or measuring cup, combine the cornstarch with the cold water. Stir until cornstarch is completely dissolved. Pour it into the syrup. Place the medium saucepan containing the syrup over medium-high heat. Using a wooden spoon or silicone spatula, stir the syrup often as it heats. After 3–4 minutes, the syrup will change from a watery consistency to a thicker, more gel-like syrup. As soon as this happens, remove from heat. Stir in the cinnamon for apple filling or the almond extract for cherry filling. Let cool for 5 minutes, then pour syrup back into fruit. Gently stir to combine. Set aside.

Make egg wash: Into a small bowl or ramekin, crack egg. Add water. Use a small fork to whisk into a light yellow liquid.

Prep dough: On a floured, flat surface, unfold one sheet of puff pastry. Use a rolling pin to smooth the surface of the dough. Use a large knife, dough cutter, or pizza cutter to cut the sheet down the middle vertically and then again horizontally. This will turn the sheet into 4 equal squares of dough.

Assemble turnovers: Onto the center of each square, spoon 2 tablespoons of filling. Brush egg wash onto all four edges of the dough. Fold one corner of the dough over the filling and line it up with the opposite corner. Press dough together along the two open sides of the turnover. Stretch the dough as needed to get the sides to line up evenly. (This may be easier if you pick up the turnover and hold it like a taco.) Once fruit filling is secured inside the turnover, place turnover onto prepped pan. Lightly brush top with egg wash. Repeat with all of the puff pastry.

Bake: Place tray in oven and bake for 20 minutes. Remove from oven. Let cool for 10 minutes. Remove from tray. Serve.

Makes 16 turnovers.

s6 e14 *Tester*—Alyssa Race

Eat Like a Gilmore DAILY CRAVINGS

RASPBERRY PEACH JAM

CONTRIBUTED BY JENNIE WHITAKER

TOWN FAVORITE

Finally, a recipe for Jackson's famous jam! There are so many tasty uses for it—spoon it over ice cream or, as Jackson himself suggests, use it to replace the marshmallows in s'mores. Or, like the photo, slather it all over pancakes. If you're into canning, you could even put some in a jar and give it as a gift—tell folks you picked it up during your recent trip to France!

The blend of these two fresh, summery fruit flavors really makes this jam a hit.

4 c	Peaches
3 c	Raspberries
2 c	Sugar
2 t	Lemon juice, freshly squeezed

Prepare fruit: Wash the peaches and raspberries in hot water with a fruit and veggie wash, or soak them in a bowl of water with vinegar for 15 minutes before use. Remove the pits from your peaches and chop the peaches into very small pieces. Smash the raspberries. *Some people prefer to blend the fruit prior to cooking for an even consistency, while others prefer a chunkier jelly.

Cook fruit: Place finely chopped and clean peaches, crushed and washed raspberries, sugar, and lemon juice in a large saucepan and cook over medium-low heat. When the sugar is dissolved and the mixture is at a full boil, allow it to cook for another 15 minutes, stirring constantly, allowing the jelly to thicken but not burn. Remove from heat.

Store jam: Using your preferred size of canning jar, carefully put the hot mixture into warmed jars and be careful not to overfill them. Let jars cool to room temperature. Store your mixture in the refrigerator for up to two weeks or put it in the freezer and it'll last up to a year. Use it on toast with butter, bagels with cream cheese, or as a topping on anything from grilled chicken to vanilla ice cream.

s1e19

ORANGE MARMALADE

CONTRIBUTED BY JENNIE WHITAKER

Luke's Diner is that place we all wish we had in our neighborhood. It's the unofficial town gathering spot, where the food is always good, the room is filled with friendly faces, and the coffee is the best around. Luke does things to make the diner a special place—but he does them quietly, without calling attention to himself. For instance, he adds new things to the menu to cater to the people he cares most about, he offers free antioxidants or free coffee when he's celebrating good news, and he goes in the kitchen to whip up fun daily specials like pumpkin pancakes when he's in a good mood. Because his establishment is a diner, it's easy to underestimate Luke's culinary abilities, but, at times, he can even keep up with Sookie.

So there's no doubt when Luke serves a side of orange marmalade with Kirk's whole wheat toast, that marmalade is made from scratch, right there in the diner; possibly by Luke, himself.

6	Red-fleshed navel oranges (Cara Cara navel recommended)
3 c	Water
3½ c	Sugar (organic recommended), *divided*
¼ c	Lemon juice, freshly squeezed
1 t	Vanilla extract

Prepare fruit: Wash the oranges in hot water with a fruit and veggie wash, or soak them in a bowl of water with vinegar for 15 minutes before use. Remove the seeds as you begin to slice the oranges. Make slices as thin as you can.

Cook fruit: Place all orange slices in a medium saucepan over medium heat. Add water, 1 cup sugar, lemon juice, and vanilla. Place a candy thermometer in pot. Bring the mixture to a boil, then turn the heat to low. Simmer mixture between 200°F and 215°F, stirring occasionally, for 30 minutes. Stir in remaining 2½ cups sugar.

Increase heat again and bring the mixture to a boil. Continue to boil mixture until thermometer reads 220°F. Remove from heat.

Store jam: Be careful not to burn yourself as you transfer the marmalade into your preferred sized canning jars and seal with lids while it's hot. Let jars cool to room temperature. Refrigerate.

Storing and serving notes: Your tart, sweet, and delicious orange marmalade can be stored in the refrigerator for up to two weeks. Put on your homemade scones and pancakes, or use as a sauce on soft cheeses, a glaze over your fruit salad, or simply eat with a spoon. Use it often and be creative.

Makes approximately 3 cups.

s7 e4

Pizza & Salad

PIZZA

AT HOME

If Lorelai and Rory subscribe to the idea of the four food groups, then pizza is definitely one of their four. They eat pizza several times a week; more if the house is undergoing renovation. Their relationship with pizza doesn't seem complicated—they don't have an uber picky go-to pizza order. They seem equally happy eating a normal cheese pizza as they are eating the largest pizza in the tristate area.

This pizza is neither delivery, nor frozen, so it's not exactly like a Gilmore version. Still, it's easy and inexpensive to make, using simple ingredients that make it a bit healthier than the average commercial pizza. Come to think of it, it's likely the kind of pizza Luke would try to introduce into the girls' lives after he moved in with Lorelai.

¾ c	Water
1 pkg	Active dry yeast
½ t	Sugar
1½ c	Flour
2 t	Kosher salt
3 T	Olive oil, plus more for bowl
1 t	Dried oregano
6 oz	Tomato sauce
3–4 c	Shredded mozzarella cheese

Bloom yeast: In a small saucepan, heat water to 100–110℉. Remove from heat. Sprinkle yeast over water. Sprinkle sugar over yeast. Let stand for 10 minutes. Watch for small bubbles and some foaming. (If neither are present, yeast is likely inactive. Discard and start again.)

Mix dough: In a medium bowl, combine flour and salt. Add yeast, oil, and oregano. Mix with a fork until a dough forms.

Proof dough: Lightly flour a flat work surface. Place dough on flour and gently knead 10–12 turns. Oil the inside of a large mixing bowl. Place dough in bowl. Cover with a clean kitchen towel. Set aside for 1 hour.

Punch down dough: Gently press the center of dough to the bottom of the bowl. Gently pull the sides of dough away from bowl, toward middle of dough. Pull dough out of bowl. Divide into two equal halves. Wrap one half in plastic wrap and refrigerate.

Prepare pan and oven: Set out a pizza pan or large baking sheet. Ensure oven rack is in center position. Preheat oven to 450°F.

Roll dough: Lightly flour a flat work surface. Place one half of dough in center. Dust top of dough with flour. Use a rolling pin to roll dough into a 13-inch circle. Place rolled dough onto pan.

Make pizza: Spoon tomato sauce onto pizza and spread it into an even layer, avoiding the outermost edge of the dough. Cover the tomato sauce with a generous layer of mozzarella cheese.

Bake pizza: Place pan in oven and bake for 10–12 minutes. Watch for cheese to be melted and beginning to brown in areas. Remove from oven. Slide pizza onto large cutting board.

Cut into 6–8 pieces. Serve.

s3 e18

Tester—Ashley Scarborough

PIZZA ROLLS

AT HOME

After a dramatic Friday Night Dinner with Emily (Richard was traveling) where Lorelai had to fight off an aggressive Christopher, the girls returned to Stars Hollow. On their way to the store, while deciding on the menu for their post-dinner food binge, they are interrupted on the sidewalk by Kirk. He calls out to Lorelai. Clearly Lorelai cannot hide any longer. She has to break it to Kirk that she won't go on a date with him.

Two men in one night who want to be with Lorelai—one, Christopher, who has a pregnant girlfriend and the other, Kirk, who is Kirk. Talk about no good options.

At least they picked up some pizza rolls.

These taste very much like their frozen counterparts, except they offer healthier ingredients, with fewer chemicals. Make a double batch. Trust me.

1	Egg
¼ c	Water
30	Wonton papers
1 can	Tomato sauce (15 ounces)
1 c	Shredded mozzarella cheese
1 c	Minced pepperoni, *optional*
2 t	Dried oregano
1 qt	Oil, for cooking (canola, vegetable, or safflower)

Make egg wash: In a small bowl or ramekin, crack egg. Add water. Use a fork to mix the two until fully combined.

Assemble pizza roll: On a flat work surface, lay out one wonton paper. Lightly brush edges with egg wash. Spoon 1 tablespoon of sauce into center of wonton paper. Top sauce with 1–2 teaspoons of cheese, 1–2 teaspoons of pepperoni, and a pinch of oregano.

Fold pizza roll: Fold squared bottom of wonton paper up toward middle of ingredients. Fold in the two sides, ensuring the egg-washed edges adhere. Fold top edge down, toward middle of pizza roll. This should cover all the ingredients in a little wonton envelope. Ensure all edges are adhering. Set aside. Repeat the assemble-and-fold step for all remaining wonton papers.

Create a drying rack: Near the stove, on a flat work surface or large cutting board, stack two paper towels. Top the paper towels with a cooling rack.

Fry pizza rolls: Heat oil in a deep skillet or Dutch oven. Use a candy thermometer to bring oil to 360°–365°F. Use a large spoon to carefully lower six pizza rolls into hot oil. Allow to cook about 2 minutes until golden brown. Use tongs or a slotted spoon to remove rolls from oil. Place them on drying rack. Repeat until all rolls are cooked. Place rolls on plate. Serve.

Makes 30 pizza rolls.

s3 e2

Tester—Cathi Kennedy

PIZZA BAGELS

When Lane eventually breaks the news to Zach that they're pregnant, Zach, being Zach, goes into full denial mode, not mentioning the baby for several days and acting like the pregnancy was never discussed at all. Lane thought Zach forgot. So, she tried jogging his memory about the baby by mentioning the cravings which would likely begin soon. Zach answered with a craving of his own—pizza bagels—then continued playing his video game.

Pizza bagels certainly are crave-worthy, but they're certainly not more important than a baby. Or two babies!

For bagels:

10 c + 2 T Water, *divided*

4 T   Barley malt syrup, *divided*

1 pkg   Active dry yeast

4 c   High-gluten flour

For 6 pizza bagels (double or triple ingredients if making more):

8 oz   Tomato sauce

1 t   Italian seasoning

½ c   Chopped pepperoni slices

2 c   Shredded mozzarella

Bloom yeast: In a saucepan over medium heat, warm 1½ cups water to 110°F. Remove from heat. Stir in 2 tablespoons of barley malt syrup. Once combined, sprinkle the full package of yeast over the top. Let rest for 10 minutes. Watch for bubbles and a light foam to appear on top of the water. These indicate the yeast is ready to use. (After 15 minutes, if no bubbling has occurred, the yeast is likely ineffective. Discard the mixture and start again.)

Mix dough: In a large mixing bowl, combine flour and salt. Pour in the yeast mixture. Using an electric hand mixer on lower speed, mix together until a dough forms. Continue to mix the dough around the bowl for 3–5 minutes to activate the gluten. Remove the dough from bowl. Prepare a flat work surface by covering it with a light layer of flour. Then knead the dough for 20 minutes. Again, this will help to activate the gluten, which will give the bagels the chewy exterior we all love!

Prepare the dough: Lightly grease the inside of a large bowl. Set dough into bowl and cover with a clean kitchen towel. Let dough rise for 1 hour. After an hour the dough should have doubled in size. Next, punch down the dough—which sounds rough, but isn't. Please continue to be gentle with your dough! Push into the center of the dough until it is deflated. Then pull the edges away from the bowl and toward the center of the dough. Prepare a lightly floured work surface again. Take the dough out of the bowl, placing it on the floured surface. Gently knead the dough for 10 turns.

Roll dough: Divide dough into 12 equal pieces. Roll each piece into a ball. Let balls rest on the work surface. Cover the dough with the kitchen towel, plastic wrap or an inverted pan to keep it from drying out. Wait 20 minutes. Your dough is now ready to use!

Prepare pan(s) and oven: Cover two baking sheets with parchment paper or a silicone baking mat. Lightly grease the parchment paper or mat with butter or oil. Set aside. Ensure oven racks are set to the center of the oven (not the top or bottom positions). Preheat oven to 425°F.

Prepare for boiling: Pour 8 cups of water into a stockpot or Dutch oven. Add the remaining 2 tablespoons of barley malt

syrup. Heat on high until boiling. While waiting for it to boil, move on to the next two steps.

Form bagels: Working with one piece at a time, poke a hole into the center of the ball using your finger. Then, with your hands, gently stretch the dough to increase the size of the hole until it's about 2 inches wide.

Boil bagels: Stack two paper towels on a plate, then place a drying rack on the paper towels. This is where you'll place the bagels after they boil. Use a spatula to lower bagels into boiling water, one at a time. Depending on the size of your pot, boil 2–4 bagels at one time. Allow bagels to boil for 2 minutes. Then remove onto the drying rack. Repeat for all.

Bake bagels: Transfer each bagel to a prepared baking sheet. Place baking sheet in oven and bake for 20 minutes. Turn bagels halfway through baking process. Bagels will be done when their tops are golden brown. Remove from oven. Let cool completely.

Assemble pizza bagels: Reduce oven to 350°F. Place a piece of parchment paper or silicone mat on a baking sheet. Cut three of the bagels in half, which will produce six "pizza crusts." Arrange crusts on pan. Slather each "crust" with tomato sauce. Sprinkle a pinch or two of Italian seasoning. Add pepperoni or other toppings as desired. Top with a generous amount of mozzarella cheese.

Bake pizza bagels: Place pan in oven. Bake for 5–6 minutes. Remove from oven. Let cool. Serve.

Store bagels: Store remaining bagels in ziplock plastic bag(s). Freeze immediately or store at room temperature. Do not refrigerate. If storing at room temperature, use within 2–3 days.

s7 e19

Tester—Devin Avellino

Eat Like a Gilmore DAILY CRAVINGS

HOTHOUSE TOMATO & HERB SALAD

This salad is deceptively simple. With so few ingredients, the success of the dish depends almost solely on the quality of the tomatoes. When an esteemed restaurant critic mentions the religious experience he had while eating your Hothouse Tomato and Herb Salad, those have to be some terrific tomatoes! Who better to have access to terrific tomatoes than Sookie? As artistic and detail-oriented as Sookie is about her food, she's met her equal in Jackson, who takes the very best care of his crops. He consistently looks for ways to improve each crop—to make them more flavorful, less dependent on summer weather, and more perfect.

With Jackson's produce as Sookie's secret weapon, it's likely she really was the very best chef; even better than Alain Ducasse.

2	Medium tomatoes, vine-ripened
1 T	Finely chopped fresh dill
2 T	Mint, fresh, torn into ¼-inch pieces
2 t	Minced parsley
¼ t	Black pepper
1 T	Lemon juice, freshly squeezed
2 t	Olive oil

Prepare tomatoes: Remove vines and stems. Wash and dry tomatoes. Cut into 1-inch cubes or wedges. Remove any hard, white core pieces. Place remaining pieces in medium bowl.

Season tomatoes: Add herbs and black pepper to tomatoes. Gently toss. Divide onto two salad plates. Drizzle each with lemon juice and olive oil. Serve.

s1 e4

THE OTHER CAESAR SALAD

When Caesar introduced *chilaquiles*, cold bananas, and chicken fingers while Luke was away, it was simply his latest attempt to inject some of his own creativity into the diner's menu. His first attempt was the salad he named after himself. Caesar was undeterred by the fact that there already is a very famous salad called "Caesar Salad." He liked his new salad and thought it could be a big hit.

He's right! This salad is a unique combination of flavors but they all work surprisingly well together. Give it a try and see if you'd order it during your next visit to Luke's.

1 head	Butter lettuce
4	Red endive
1 batch	Guacamole (see page 71)
1 T	Crushed red pepper
2	Lemons, cut into wedges
	Cilantro, as garnish

Prepare ingredients: Wash and dry butter lettuce and endive. Tear butter lettuce leaves into 2-inch pieces. Cut the bottoms off the endives. Cut endives lengthwise into thin wedges.

Assemble salad: Cover a salad plate or the bottom of a salad bowl with butter lettuce leaves. Top with endive pieces. Scoop roughly 3 tablespoons of guacamole onto the center of salad.

Garnish salad: Sprinkle a pinch or two of red pepper, distributing it around entire surface. Place two wedges of lemon on side of plate. Top the guacamole with a few chopped leaves of cilantro. Repeat for as many servings as needed.

Makes 8 individual salads.

POTATO SALAD

In the "Grossest Male Character" contest, we have two major contenders—both related to Jackson! Jackson's cousin, Rune, and Jackson's brother, Beau. Rune is unbelievably rude to Lorelai, selfish and needy toward Jackson, and uncouth enough to change his pants in the kitchen at the Inn.

However, the truly grossest male character is Beau. When he gets it into his head that Lorelai is a nymphomaniac, his resulting behavior takes the award, no contest. Remember him licking his key? How about at the baby shower when he utters the words "potato" and "salad" in the creepiest way imaginable.

Fortunately, this Potato Salad tastes so good it'll neutralize its bad Beau association. It'll also help you forget Lorelai's horrible behavior during the baptism ceremony.

6	Russet potatoes, peeled, halved
1 T	Salt
6	Eggs, hard-boiled, cold, peeled
1 c	Peeled and finely chopped onion
¾ c	Finely chopped celery (2 large stalks)
⅓ c	Very thinly sliced radish
2 t	Kosher salt
2 t	Black pepper
½ t	Cayenne pepper
1 c	Mayonnaise
1 T	Yellow mustard
2 t	Lemon juice, freshly squeezed
	Paprika, sweet, garnish
	Parsley, garnish

Boil potatoes: Place potato halves in a stockpot or Dutch oven. Fill pot with cold water until water covers potatoes. Bring potatoes to a boil over high heat. Add salt. Reduce heat just enough to keep water gently bubbling. Boil for approximately 10 minutes. Cooking the potatoes to the proper doneness is very important to the success of the dish.

Test for doneness: After 8 minutes, test the potatoes by inserting a fork into the center of one potato. If it feels hard or gritty at all, the potato is not yet done. When you poke a potato and it is done, it will feel soft, smooth, and velvety. Remove from heat immediately and either strain the water out or remove the potatoes one by one with tongs and place them in a bowl. Cool potatoes to room temperature.

Cube potatoes: Once potatoes have cooled to room temperature, cut them into cubes about ¾ inch by ¾ inch. Place cubed potatoes in a large mixing bowl.

Slice and chop eggs: Slice eggs in thin circles. Take six of the largest, prettiest circles and set them aside to use as garnish. From the remaining egg slices, remove yolks and place them in a medium bowl. You'll have a pile of cooked egg whites left over. Chop them up and add them to the potatoes.

Add vegetables and spices: Add onion, celery, radishes, kosher salt, and both peppers to potatoes. Set aside.

Make dressing: With a fork, mash egg yolks in medium bowl. Add mayonnaise, mustard, and lemon juice. Mix until dressing is smooth, fully combined, and a creamy yellow color. Use a silicone spatula to scrape all dressing onto the top of the potatoes. Use same spatula to gently fold the dressing into the potatoes.

Garnish and serve: Once all dressing has been mixed evenly into potatoes, top potatoes with the 6 egg slices. Garnish with parsley. Sprinkle with paprika. This may be served immediately. However, it is recommended to cover with plastic wrap or aluminum foil and refrigerate for 2 hours prior to serving.

Makes 10–12 servings.

s6 e4

EGGLESS EGG SALAD

Everyone loves the dance marathon! The costumes, the hairstyles, the dancing—it's one of the very best town events of the entire series. They dance for twenty-four hours straight, with only brief breaks to rest and recharge.

Did you ever wonder, why in the world are Mrs. Kim's Eggless Egg Sandwiches the only food available? Luke is already there—why wasn't he serving food?

At least people seemed to enjoy the sandwiches—especially Dave, who really proved himself as great boyfriend material when he lavished praise on Mrs. Kim for her sandwiches.

His praise was likely genuine—these sandwiches taste very much like egg salad, without having to boil any eggs!

8 oz	Tofu block, firm or extra firm
2 T	Dill relish
2 T	Minced green onion
1 t	Minced fresh dill weed
2 T	Vegan mayonnaise
1 T	Rice wine vinegar
1 t	Prepared yellow mustard
½ t	Salt
½ t	Black pepper
1½ t	Ground turmeric

Prepare tofu: Place tofu in a doubled or tripled piece of cheesecloth. Squeeze to remove as much liquid as possible. Place tofu in medium mixing bowl. Add relish, onion, and dill weed. Set aside.

Make dressing: In small bowl or ramekin, combine mayonnaise, vinegar, mustard, salt, and pepper. Stir to combine.

Make eggless egg salad: Scoop dressing into tofu mixture. Stir well to combine fully. Add the turmeric in half-teaspoon increments. It will turn the mixture a pleasing "egg yolk yellow." Continue to add it until the mixture reaches your desired color.

Serve: Spread on bread or toast, or scoop onto a green salad. Serve.

s3e7

CHICKEN SALAD
CONTRIBUTED BY TONY ESCARCEGA

After Rory swapped Dean for Jess at the dance marathon, the tensions between the two young men intensified, understandably. The town suddenly seemed too small for the both of them. With Jess working at Luke's and Dean helping out Tom, it was impossible for the two to avoid interacting with one another.

When Dean entered Luke's and placed the large order for all of Tom's crew, consisting of multiple burgers, multiple hot dogs, a few salads, and various sandwiches—including one chicken salad sandwich—Jess thought Dean was pranking him. He wasn't. Somehow, they managed to get the order placed, but having to deal with one another like that must have posed a real dilemma for both of them.

The only dilemma for us is, why was the chicken salad only ordered by one person? This chicken salad is incredible!

For chicken:

¼ c	Olive oil
4	Split bone-in, skin-on chicken breasts (equivalent of 2 whole breasts),

For salad:

1 c	Peeled and diced red onion
1½ c	Finely chopped celery
1 c + 2 T	Mayonnaise
2 t	Dijon mustard
2 T	Miracle Whip, *optional*
1 T	Lemon juice, freshly squeezed
1 t	Salt
1 t	Black pepper
2	Apples, medium, cored and chopped (Fuji recommended)
1 c	Red grapes, halved if large, whole if small

Prepare pan and oven: Place a sheet of aluminum foil on a baking sheet. Set aside. Place oven rack in center position. Preheat oven to 350°F.

Roast chicken: Rub olive oil on chicken breasts and sprinkle with salt and pepper. Place chicken in pan and pan in oven. Roast for 35–40 minutes or until done. To test doneness, insert instant-read thermometer. When chicken reaches 165°F, it's done. Set aside and let cool.

Mix salad: In a large mixing bowl, combine red onion, celery, mayonnaise, mustard, Miracle Whip (if using), and lemon juice. Put in refrigerator to chill.

Chop or shred chicken: Once chicken is cool to the touch, remove skin and bone. Chop the chicken into bite size pieces or shred with two forks. Add chicken to salad. Add salt, pepper, apples, and grapes.

Serve: If needed, chicken salad may be served immediately. Ideally, cover and refrigerate for 4 hours before serving.

Serving ideas: May be used as sandwich filling, slider filling, or topping for green salad. May also be served with crackers or tortilla chips.

Chinese Take-Out
Favorites

EGG ROLLS

In this scene, Rory walks to Al's to pick up the Chinese food Lorelai ordered. On her way back home, she runs into Jess. Sure, she and Jess have spoken before, but not like this. This encounter marks the first time we see mutual sexual tension between the two of them. During the encounter they discuss books, literary characters, and reading, but as Rory's T-shirt says, "Reading is Sexy." At least Rory and Jess seem to make it so.

As they part, and Jess tells Rory she owes him an eggroll, we know he's talking about a lot more than food.

2 T	Sesame oil
½ c	Minced green onion
3 T	Minced fresh ginger
2 T	Minced fresh garlic
2 c	Finely chopped chicken thigh meat
3 T	Soy sauce
2 T	Orange juice, freshly squeezed
1 T	Sugar
2 c	Thinly sliced, then chopped, red cabbage
1 c	Peeled, thinly sliced, then chopped, carrot
1 c	Chopped bok choy leaves and stems
2 c	Bean sprouts
1	Egg
2 t	Water
20	Egg roll wrappers
	Peanut oil, for frying

Note: Prep all ingredients before beginning to cook.

Make filling: In a deep skillet, Dutch oven, or wok, add sesame oil over high heat. Allow oil to heat 2–3 minutes, until it moves easily around the pan to coat it. Add green onion, ginger, and garlic. Sauté for 2–3 minutes. Mix in the chicken. Cook chicken for 2–3 minutes, until meat begins to turn from pink to white. Add soy sauce and orange juice, then sprinkle with sugar. Mix and continue to sauté. Once meat is cooked through, add cabbage, carrot, and bok choy. Mix well. Once vegetables are wilted (about 2 minutes), remove from heat and mix in bean sprouts. This is your filling.

Make egg wash: In a small bowl or ramekin, crack the egg, then add water and beat with a fork until egg and water are mixed. It will take on a milky appearance.

Wrap egg rolls: Place each wrapper in front of you with one corner pointing toward you. Measure ½ cup of filling and place onto the wrapper about 2 inches in from the corner closest to you. Flip that corner up and over the filling. Brush a thin, light layer of egg wash along the two farthest edges (this will help keep the wrapping closed during frying). Fold in both sides—the two points should meet in the middle. Then roll the filled side of the wrapper toward the farthest corner. Voilà! Follow the same method for the remaining 19 egg rolls.

Prepare to fry egg rolls: Fill a deep skillet, Dutch oven, or wok with peanut oil, until oil is 2 inches deep. Heat oil over high heat until it reaches 360–375°F (use a candy thermometer to check temperature). While oil is heating, cover a baking sheet or large cutting board with two layers of paper towel. Place one large or two small wire cooling racks over the paper towel. Use this to drain the egg rolls when they come out of the oil. Also, use long-handled tongs or a long-handled slotted spoon to manage the egg rolls while they are in the oil. The long handle will allow you to stand away from the oil, in case it pops or splatters.

Fry egg rolls: Get out two large bowls and a slotted spoon. Fill one bowl halfway with cold/ice water. Once water in the pot is boiling, add broccoli pieces to the pot. Cook broccoli for 2 minutes only. Use the slotted spoon to remove broccoli from boiling water and place into the cold water. Once all broccoli is in the cold water, use slotted spoon to remove the broccoli from the cold water and place it in the empty bowl. Remove water from heat and discard. Also discard the cold water.

Serve: Serve with dipping sauce of choice.

Wrapped, unfried egg rolls may be frozen in a ziplock plastic bag, then taken out later, thawed, and fried.

Tester—Sarah Panizza

Eat Like a Gilmore DAILY CRAVINGS

POT STICKERS

We fans love to have our attention captured by the girls' romantic relationships. But if we stand back and analyze all of Lorelai's and Rory's, and even Emily's, episodes of breaking up and getting back together with Max, Christopher, Luke, Dean, Logan, and Richard, it becomes apparent, that Gilmore girls tend to have rather chaotic love lives! Some of that chaos extends into friendship, as well. For instance, the same break up/get back together element is present in Rory's friendship with Paris (though the drama is mostly caused by Paris).

Very shortly after dramatically leaving all of Rory's belongings out on the landing, suddenly the two become chummy again when Rory shows up, drunk, at the door. They've both broken up with their boyfriends so they are both hurting. Paris makes a complete turnaround by welcoming Rory back into the apartment—to live. Then the two sit and plan all of the fun decorating they will do to the apartment, while sharing a load of Chinese food. They even toast by clinking Rory's bite of chicken with Paris's pot sticker.

Make up a batch of these and toast to all of the plans you have in the works—no chaos required.

For pot stickers:

2½ c	Finely chopped cabbage
½ lb	Ground pork
¼ c	Minced green onions, white parts only
1½ T	Peeled and minced fresh ginger
1 T	Peeled and minced garlic
1 T	Soy sauce
2 t	Toasted sesame oil
¼ t	White pepper
⅛ t	Black pepper
30	Pot sticker/dumpling wrappers
¼ c	Oil, for frying (canola, vegetable, or safflower)
½ c	Water

For sauce:

2 T	Soy sauce
1 T	White vinegar or rice vinegar
½ t	Crushed red pepper
¼ c	Cold water
2 T	Cornstarch

Mix filling: In large bowl, combine cabbage, pork, green onions, ginger, and garlic. Add soy sauce, sesame oil, salt, and peppers. Mix thoroughly to combine. This is your filling.

Stuff dumplings: Lightly flour a large plate, flat pan, or cutting board. Set aside. Place one pot sticker wrapper on the floured work surface. Spoon 2 teaspoons of filling into middle of wrapper. Dip finger in the 2 tablespoons of water, then run it around the outer edge of wrapper to moisten. Fold wrapper so edges meet up. Fold the edge into 5–6 pleats. Set pot sticker on floured plate. Repeat until all filling has been used.

Fry pot stickers: Choose a deep skillet, large frying pan, or Dutch oven—something with a tight-fitting lid. Over medium-high heat, heat oil until it is very hot, but not yet smoking. Reduce heat to low. Arrange all 30 pot stickers, standing up, close together. Let them cook for 2–3 minutes, until dark golden brown on the bottom.

Steam pot stickers: Remove from heat. Add ½ cup water. Cover the pan with lid and wait 7–8 minutes. (Lift lid halfway through to make sure water is evaporating—if water is not evaporating, return pan to low heat.) Once all water has evaporated, remove lid. Flip pot stickers with a fork or a strong flick of the wrist to unstick them from the pan. Let them rest in pan 2 minutes, then dump them out onto a plate.

Make optional sauce: In a small bowl or ramekin, combine all ingredients and stir. Serve pot stickers with sauce.

Makes 30 pot stickers.

s6 e17

FRIED RICE

Marty and Rory have their movie marathon interrupted by Logan, who invites them out for dinner. They go. Rory seems casual, comfortably enjoying her meal with Logan and the gang. Marty clearly feels awkward and uncomfortable the entire time—partly from being surrounded by a bunch of guys he doesn't really like and partly because he knows the ATM is going to flip him off when he tries to withdraw money to pay for dinner. Why did you agree to go, Marty?

Marty could have easily just made this fried rice at home. He would've saved himself the misery, and seventy-five bucks. Don't be like Marty.

2 T	Butter
2	Garlic cloves, peeled and minced
1 c	Bite-size pieces of chicken thigh meat
½ t	Black pepper
¼ c + 1½ t	Soy sauce, *divided*
⅓ c	Minced green onion
½ c	Frozen carrot slices, thawed
½ c	Frozen baby peas, thawed
2	Eggs
2–3 T	Vegetable oil
2½ c	Cooked medium-grain rice, (a day old or more, recommended)
2 T	Sherry
	Cilantro, garnish, *optional*

Note: Prep all ingredients before beginning to cook.

Cook chicken: In a large frying pan or wok, melt butter over high heat. Add garlic and chicken. To ensure meat gets cooked evenly, use wooden spoon or spatula to flip every 30 seconds. Sprinkle with pepper and 1½ teaspoons of soy sauce. Once chicken pieces are lightly browned on all sides and garlic smells fragrant (4–5 minutes), use a slotted spoon to remove mixture from pan and place into a bowl. Set aside. Leave liquids in bottom of pan.

Cook vegetables: With heat remaining on high, add the green onion, carrots, and peas to the remaining liquids. Mix the vegetables every 30 seconds to cook them evenly. Once onion is translucent and carrots begin to show a slight bit of browning around the edges, use a slotted spoon to remove vegetables from pan. Place them into a bowl. Set aside. Leave any liquids in bottom of pan.

Boil water: In a large saucepan or Dutch oven, bring 8–10 cups of water to a rolling boil.

Cook egg: With heat still set to high setting, crack each egg directly into pan. Quickly use a spatula to break the yolks and stir eggs a bit. Allow eggs to cook for 15–20 seconds in between using spatula to mix and flip them. Once eggs are cooked, remove them from pan and place them in bowl. Set aside.

Fry rice: With heat still set to high, add vegetable oil to pan. Wait 30 seconds, then add rice to pan. Allow rice to fry in oil for about a minute. Then flip the rice, using a spatula. Pour ¼ cup soy sauce and sherry evenly across rice. Use spatula to mix the liquids into the rice until color is even. Add chicken, vegetables, and egg. Mix well. Allow mixture to cook 2 more minutes, flipping rice every 10–15 seconds.

Serve: Remove from heat. Spoon rice mixture out of pan onto one large serving dish or individual dishes. Garnish with cilantro, if desired. Serve.

Makes 5 cups.

Tester—Nicole Krieger-Loos

SWEET-AND-SOUR PORK

TOWN FAVORITE

Remember that "Scene in a Mall"? We can't deny the excitement we all get after a long day at the mall when we walk into the food court and are taken aback by the aromas of cafeteria-style foods.

After Emily's meltdown in the mall, Lorelai and Rory treat her to that alluring smorgasbord of food court delicacies. Throughout the series, the girls are never without their Chinese food. So, it's not a surprise when we see them bring over Sweet-and-Sour Pork. Overwhelmed with options, Emily starts off with the Orange Julius.

Pair this Sweet-and-Sour Pork with an Orange Julius, and you've got the perfect combination to 'couch potato' it. Save yourself a trip window shopping. Turn on some *Gilmore Girls* and cook up this delicious meal! It's the perfect excuse to play hooky.

Pork:

¼ c	Soy sauce
1 T	Brown sugar
2 T	Minced green onion
1 lb	Pork loin, cubed
1½ c	Cornstarch
1½	quarts vegetable oil

Sweet-and-Sour Sauce:

1 c	Water
4 oz	Tomato paste
¼ c	Brown sugar
2 T	Unseasoned rice vinegar
3 T	Soy sauce
¾ c	Pineapple juice (drained from can of pineapple chunks)
¼ c	Cold water
2 T	Cornstarch

Vegetables:

2 T	Butter
1	Green bell pepper, seeds removed, julienned
1	Medium yellow onion, coarsely chopped
2	Carrots, peeled, julienned

Prepare pork: In medium bowl, combine ¼ cup soy sauce, 1 tablespoon brown sugar, green onion, and cubed pork loin. Set aside. Pour oil into Dutch oven or stockpot. Using a candy thermometer to measure, over high heat, bring oil to 375°F. Prepare a place with two sheets of paper towel on it. Set aside.

Cook pork: Pour 1½ cups cornstarch into shallow bowl. One by one, remove each piece of pork from its marinade and dip it into cornstarch, turning to coat on all sides. Carefully place each piece into hot oil. Placing the meat into the oil may dip its temperature. Ensure the temperature remains between 350 and 375°F. Cook each piece until the outside is golden brown. Using a slotted or straining spoon, remove the done pieces and place them on the plate with the paper towel. When all pieces are cooked, remove oil from heat.

Make sauce: In medium saucepan, combine 1 cup water and tomato paste. Begin to heat the mixture using medium-high heat. Stir to dissolve the paste. Add brown sugar, vinegar, soy sauce, and pineapple juice. Stir. If sauce begins to boil, reduce heat. Allow to simmer for 8–10 minutes.

Thicken sauce: Pour ¼ cup cold water into a small bowl or ramekin. Sprinkle 2 tablespoons of cornstarch into water. Using a fork, stir the cornstarch until it is fully dissolved in the water. The mixture will take on a milky consistency. Stir it into the sweet-and-sour sauce. Continue stirring sauce until it begins to thicken. Stir in pork. Remove from heat. Set aside.

Cook vegetables: In a deep skillet or wok, add butter. Over high heat, melt the butter, then add vegetables. Sauté, flipping vegetables every minute or so, for 5–6 minutes. Once onions are translucent and carrots are pliable, add pork mixture to pan. Carefully mix until vegetables are fully incorporated.

Serve over rice.

s4 e15

INTRO BY DEIDRA LONG
Tester—Nicole Krieger-Loos

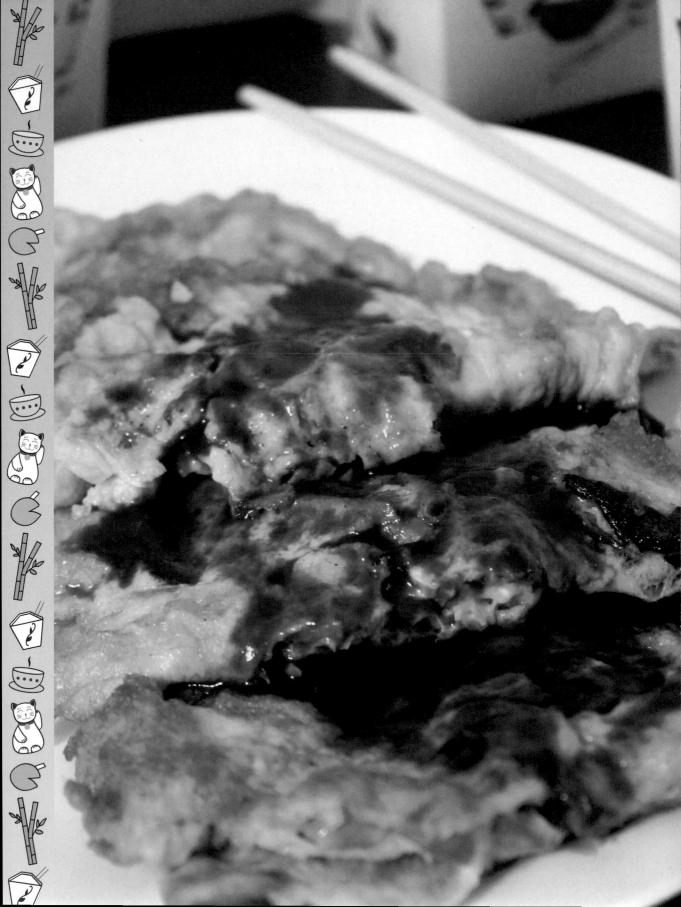

EGG FOO YOUNG

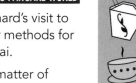
AL'S PANCAKE WORLD

An unemployed Richard is a bored and annoying Richard. We learned this during Richard's visit to Stars Hollow. With critical comments about Lorelai's breakfast, her work attire, and her methods for managing the Inn, Richard started in with nitpicking early in the day, all aimed at Lorelai.

So, later on, it is understandable when Lorelai explodes. Richard's interference in the matter of Rory's car results in an abrupt end to the visit. Thankfully, she still ordered a heap of Chinese food from Al's, including the best egg foo young to be found in Stars Hollow.

Poor Richard didn't get any Chinese food. Then, again, did he really deserve it?

6–8 oz	Chicken meat, chopped
1 t	Soy sauce
1 t	Sherry
1⅛ t	Kosher salt, *divided*
¼ t	Sugar
¼ c	Vegetable oil
3 T	Chopped green onion (use white and green parts)
3 T	Julienned carrots
3 T	Chopped cabbage
2 T	Cold water
1 T	Cornstarch
5	Eggs

Sauce:

3 T	Soy sauce
2 T	Hoisin sauce
2 T	Sherry

Prep chicken: In medium bowl, combine chicken, soy sauce, sherry, ⅛ teaspoon kosher salt, and sugar. Use a spoon or spatula to combine. Let stand for 5–10 minutes.

Cook chicken: In deep skillet, Dutch oven, or wok, heat 2 tablespoons of vegetable oil over high heat. Move pan around to coat bottom with oil. Add chicken to pan. Use slotted spoon to spread chicken evenly around pan. Turn chicken every 30–45 seconds to cook it evenly on all sides. Once the color has changed from pink to white on all sides, use slotted spoon to remove chicken from pan. Place it in a clean, medium bowl. Let cool for 10 minutes.

Prep vegetables: In another medium bowl, combine green onion, carrots, and cabbage. Set aside.

Prep cornstarch: Pour cold water into a small bowl or ramekin. Add cornstarch. Stir with a fork until cornstarch is dissolved completely.

Make sauce: In a small bowl, combine soy sauce, hoisin sauce, and sherry. Mix thoroughly.

Prep eggs: Crack eggs into a large bowl. Add 1 teaspoon kosher salt. Add cornstarch liquid. Lightly whisk eggs. Add chicken and vegetables to eggs. Gently mix all ingredients together.

Prep paper towels: Place a large plate, cutting board, or small cookie sheet near the stove. Top with 2 layers of paper towel.

Fry egg mixture: Add 2 tablespoons vegetable oil to same pan in which the chicken was cooked. Heat oil over high heat. Once oil is hot, reduce heat to medium-high. Using a ladle or measuring cup, ladle roughly 1 cup of the egg mixture into the oil. Mixture will form a sort of ragged edge pancake in pan. Allow to cook for about a minute. Use a spatula to loosen the egg from the bottom of the pan on all sides. Then flip the egg over so it can cook on the other side. After 1 minute, remove egg from pan and place on paper towels. Repeat this step until all batter has been fried.

Serve: Arrange pancakes on a plate with sauce either on the side or poured over top. Serve.

s2e12 **Tester**—Lauren Cutrone

GARLIC CHICKEN

In many ways, *Gilmore Girls* teaches us how to insert fun and imagination into mundane, day-to-day things. For instance, when ordering Chinese food, why not order the entire chicken column? It turns a meal into a fun adventure! Plus, you may get to try some things you've never tried before.

For certain, this garlic chicken will be on the list, and who knows, it may turn into your new favorite dish.

1 lb	Chicken thighs, boneless, skinless
1 T	Cornstarch
1 T	Sesame oil
1 T	Rice vinegar
¼ c + 1 T	Soy sauce, *divided*
¼ t	White pepper
2 T	Oil, vegetable
6	Garlic cloves, peeled, minced
1 T	Peeled and minced fresh ginger
10	Scallions, white parts, cut into 1-inch pieces
2 T	Sherry
1 t	Sugar
	Cooked rice, for serving, *optional*

Marinate chicken: Cut chicken into chunks. Place chunks in medium bowl. Sprinkle with cornstarch. Add sesame oil, rice vinegar, 1 tablespoon soy sauce, and white pepper. Mix all ingredients. Let stand at room temperature for 10 minutes.

Fry vegetables: Heat oil in wok, Dutch oven, or deep skillet over high heat. Test oil to make sure it's hot enough by adding a couple tiny pieces of garlic. When oil sizzles around garlic, it's ready. Add garlic, ginger, and scallions to oil. Sauté for 1 minute.

Make garlic chicken: Add chicken to vegetables. Stir-fry until chicken has all turned white. Add sherry and stir to evaporate. Sprinkle sugar over chicken. Add ¼ cup soy sauce. Stir to combine. Remove from heat.

Serve over rice.

s2 e15

KUNG PAO CHICKEN

While getting ready for Rory's coming-out ball, Christopher, Dean, Lorelai, and Rory all huddle in the girls' living room, making sure they have all of their attire and teaching Rory how to act like a "lady." One very ladylike trait Lorelai tries to pass on is spitting the peanuts back into the container of Kung Pao Chicken. If only Emily could have been there to see it.

¼ c + 1 T	Soy sauce, *divided*
2 T	Chili garlic sauce or chili sauce
1 T	Honey
1 t	Rice vinegar
1½ T	Sesame oil
2 c	Cubed boneless chicken, thigh, or breast
2 T	Cornstarch
3 T	Peanut oil, *divided*
2 T	Sherry
1 c	Coarsely chopped green onion (use white and green parts)
1 T	Peeled and minced garlic
2 T	Peeled and minced ginger
15	Small dried peppers
1 T	Szechuan peppercorns
¾ c	Dry-roasted, unsalted peanuts
1	Green bell pepper, stem and seeds removed, julienned, *optional*

Note: Prep all ingredients before beginning to cook.

Make sauce: In medium bowl, combine ¼ cup soy sauce, chili sauce, honey, rice vinegar, and sesame oil. Whisk together. Set aside.

Prepare chicken: Place cubed chicken into medium bowl. Add 1 tablespoon soy sauce. Mix to coat. Add cornstarch. Mix to coat.

Heat oil: Pour 2 tablespoons of peanut oil into a wok, deep skillet, or Dutch oven over high heat. After 2 minutes, move the pan around until the bottom is coated with oil. The oil needs to be very hot when you add the chicken. To test if the oil is hot enough, dip a wooden spoon in it. If there are bubbles around the wood, the oil is ready.

Cook chicken: Add chicken. Sauté for 3–4 minutes, turning pieces in order to cook them on all sides. Once chicken is almost fully cooked, use a slotted spoon to remove chicken from pan. Place chicken in a medium bowl and set aside.

Cook vegetables: While pan is still over high heat, add sherry. Add 1 tablespoon peanut oil. Allow it to heat for a minute or two. Then add green onion, garlic, ginger, and dried peppers to pan. Sauté for 2–3 minutes.

Assemble: Add the sauce to the pan and stir until vegetables are evenly coated. Add chicken and do the same. Finally, add peanuts (and green pepper, if using). Give it all a good stir to fully mix all of the ingredients.

Makes 3 cups.

s2 e6   **Tester**—Nicole Krieger-Loos

CHICKEN IN BROWN SAUCE

Per Rory's direct request, Lorelai decides to try making nice with Jess. While he's on the roof cleaning out the rain gutters, Lorelai goes into the kitchen to get herself some leftover Chinese food for lunch. She then pauses and we know she's remembering Rory's request. So, she goes outside and invites Jess to eat with her.

Jess immediately declines the offer. But, Rory had also directly requested for Jess to make an effort with her mother. We clearly see Jess recall Rory's request before he changes his mind and accepts Lorelai's request.

The two share several dishes from the chicken column and manage to have a friendly conversation. Granted, it all goes south later, when Lorelai catches Jess leaving Rory's room. But for a few minutes, there was peace.

No chicken column is complete without Chicken in Brown Sauce—it's a staple dish. The brown sauce is an all-purpose gravy in Chinese cooking. It's the foundation for dishes like Chicken with Broccoli, Beef with Broccoli, and General Tso's Chicken.

Sauce:

1 lb	Chicken thigh meat, cut into 1-inch pieces
1 T	Rice wine vinegar
2 T	Soy sauce
2 T	Oyster sauce
2 T	Cornstarch

For stir-fry:

2 T	Water
1 T	Cornstarch
2 T	Oil
4	Garlic cloves
8	Green onions, white parts only, coarsely chopped
2 T	Sherry
¼ c	Soy sauce
1 T	Sesame oil
½ c	Dried red pepper pods

Marinate meat: In medium bowl combine chicken pieces, rice wine vinegar, soy sauce, oyster sauce, and cornstarch. Stir to combine. Let sit for 10 minutes.

Prepare cornstarch: In a small bowl or ramekin, combine 2 tablespoons cold water plus 1 tablespoon cornstarch. Stir until fully dissolved. Set aside.

Stir-fry: In a wok or Dutch oven, heat oil over high heat. When very hot, add garlic and onion. Stirring often so they don't burn, cook garlic and onions until they are golden brown. Add chicken and cook until all sides of chicken turn from pink to white. Add sherry and soy sauce. Stir to combine. Add prepared cornstarch. Stir until sauce begins to thicken. Add sesame oil and pepper pods. Remove from heat. Serve over rice.

s2 e15

Tester—Rebecca Broomall

Essential Mexican Foods

BREAKFAST QUESADILLA

Technically, Luke moved in with Nicole, aka his wife. However, he keeps sleeping in his apartment above the diner. Plus, he and Nicole have been fighting, off and on, for days.

Meanwhile, he recently gave Lorelai $30,000 to help with Dragonfly. He's also been making her a special breakfast quesadilla each morning, taking time to give it just the right ratio of Jack-cheese-to-cheddar-cheese.

Does something smell fishy?

4	Bacon slices
2	Eggs
3 T	Peeled and finely chopped red onion
1 T	Stemmed and minced jalapeño
½ T	Butter
2	Tortillas, burrito size
1 c	Shredded Monterey Jack cheese
1 c	Shredded cheddar cheese
2 T	Minced cilantro
	Salsa, for serving, *optional*
	Sour cream, for serving, *optional*

Fry bacon: Stack 2 paper towels on a flat work surface, or a plate. Set aside. Place frying pan on burner. Add bacon to pan in single layer, with slices next to each other, but with a tiny bit of space between them. Turn on the heat to medium. Heat frying pan over medium-high heat. After 2–3 minutes, turn bacon slices using tongs or a fork. Cook for 1–2 more minutes, until bacon is crispy. Remove pan from heat. Let bacon sit 1–2 additional minutes. Remove bacon slices from pan and place on the paper towels. Leave remaining bacon grease in pan. Return pan to stove.

Fry eggs: Crack eggs into a medium mixing bowl. Use a fork to scramble them together lightly. Set aside. Heat bacon grease over medium heat for 1–2 minutes. Add onion and jalapeño, stirring often. Let onion and jalapeño cook for 1 minute, then pour in eggs. Use a silicone spatula or wooden spoon to gently scramble eggs one time in pan, ensuring all loose, liquid egg comes into contact with the bottom of the pan. As soon as all egg has cooked lightly, remove from heat. Spoon eggs into a bowl. Set aside. Once the frying pan has cooled enough to touch it, use paper towels to wipe out the inside. Return pan to stove.

Make quesadilla: Over medium heat, melt butter in frying pan. Ensure melted butter covers bottom of pan. Place one tortilla in the pan, so it covers the bottom without curving or curling. Working quickly but carefully, cover the tortilla in the pan with half the Monterey Jack and half the cheddar cheese. Add bacon slices and eggs so both are evenly distributed. Top with remaining cheeses and cilantro. Place second tortilla on top. Continue to cook for 1–2 minutes. Peek under the bottom tortilla every 30 seconds to make sure it's not burning. When it reaches a beautiful golden brown color, use a large spatula to flip it. Keep heat on for 1 minute. Then turn heat off and allow quesadilla to continue to cook in pan for 2–3 minutes.

Serve: Remove from pan. Use a large knife or pizza slicer to cut into 6 or 8 wedges. Serve with salsa and sour cream.

Makes 2–4 servings.

s4 e16   **Tester**—Cathi Kennedy

HARD TACOS

The Stars Hollow Museum opens in the old Twickham House, and suddenly Lorelai must feel like she's opened an Adult Day Care. She has Rory and Paris staying with her, drunk off Founders' Day Punch. She also has Kirk staying there, who gets sugar drunk off Abba Zabbas. The next morning Lorelai gets up early and makes a run to get hangover food for the three of them—lots of it.

For chicken/pollo asado:

2 lb	Bone-in, skin-on chicken breasts (may substitute 1 lb thighs, skinless, boneless)
1 T	Kosher salt
1 T	Black pepper
¼ c	Olive oil
4–6	Garlic cloves, peeled, crushed
½	Onion, peeled, sliced into thin strips
½ c	Orange juice, freshly squeezed
2 T	Lemon juice, freshly squeezed
1 T	Lime juice, freshly squeezed
1 t	Crushed red pepper
1 t	Dried oregano
1 t	Paprika, sweet (not smoked)
1 t	Ground cumin
½ t	Ground coriander
½ t	Cayenne pepper
¼ c	Water

For tacos:

¼ c	Oil
6	Corn tortillas
3 c	Shredded lettuce
1½ c	Chopped tomato
2 c	Shredded cheese, cheddar or Monterey Jack
	Salsa, *optional*
	Sour cream, *optional*
	Guacamole, *optional* (recipe on page 71)

Rub chicken: Wash chicken and pat dry with paper towels. In a small bowl, combine salt and pepper. Rub chicken with the salt and pepper mixture. Let chicken stand for 10 minutes.

Marinate chicken: Add all remaining ingredients to a glass bowl or a large ziplock plastic bag. Mix thoroughly. Add chicken pieces and submerge. Either cover bowl with plastic wrap or zip the plastic bag closed. Refrigerate overnight (4 hours minimum).

Cook chicken (choose method):

Grill: Using an outdoor barbeque grill, heat grill, then place chicken on hot grill. Grill for 4–5 minutes per side. The outside should be medium to dark brown and seared, but not burned. Remove from grill. Let stand 10 minutes.

Broil: If your broiler is in your oven, ensure oven rack is in the position second from top. Turn on broiler. Cover a baking sheet with aluminum foil, shiny-side down. Arrange chicken on baking sheet in a single layer with no overlapping. Place pan in broiler for 10 minutes. Remove pan, turn chicken, then place pan back in broiler for another 10 minutes. Remove pan and let stand for 10 minutes.

Roast: Ensure oven rack is in center position. Preheat oven to 400°. Cover a baking sheet with aluminum foil, shiny-side down. Arrange chicken on baking sheet in a single layer with no overlapping. Place pan in oven. Roast chicken for 30–40 minutes (start checking after 20–25 minutes). Remove pan and let stand for 10 minutes.

Set up drying rack: Stack two paper towels on a plate or cutting board. Place a wire cooling rack on top of the paper towels. Place plate or cutting board near stove.

Fry tortillas: In a large frying pan or a Dutch oven, heat oil over high heat for 3–4 minutes. Tear off a small bit of tortilla and add it to oil. If it sizzles, the oil is ready. Add 1 tortilla to oil. After 25–30 seconds, use tongs to turn over tortilla. Immediately use tongs to fold tortilla in half, frying the shell for 10–15 seconds per side. When done, remove from oil immediately and place on drying rack. Repeat for remaining tortillas.

Shred chicken: Using two forks, remove skin from chicken breasts and discard. Use forks to pull meat from bone. Place meat in shallow bowl or on a plate. While using one fork to hold down a piece of meat, use the second fork to shred the meat. Repeat until all meat has been shredded.

Assemble tacos: Divide meat into 6 equal portions. Fill each tortilla shell with one portion of chicken. Garnish with lettuce, tomatoes, and cheese. Repeat for all tortilla shells. Serve with salsa, sour cream, and guacamole.

Makes 6 tacos.

Tester—Devin Avellino

Eat Like a Gilmore DAILY CRAVINGS

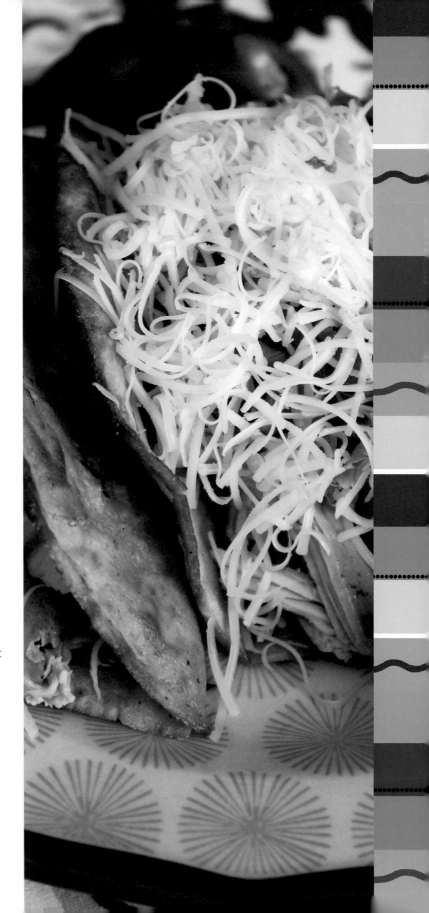

SOFT TACOS MADE WITH CARNE ASADA

TOWN FAVORITE

As Rory gets ready for her first Chilton dance, Sookie drops by with some tacos and burritos. She knows her girls well! Later, when Emily drops by and wants to take pictures of Rory in her dress, Rory emerges from the kitchen with a napkin hanging from her dress and a taco in her hand. Doesn't that sound like the perfect pre-dance photo? Emily didn't think so.

For carne asada:

1 lb	Flank steak (flap steak or skirt steak may be substituted)
1	Stemmed and chopped jalapeño pepper
3	Garlic cloves, peeled, minced
1 T	Ground cumin
2 t	Black pepper
2 t	Kosher salt
1 t	Chili powder
½ t	Cinnamon
½ c	Chopped fresh cilantro
½ c	Orange juice, freshly squeezed
¼ c	Lemon juice, freshly squeezed
2 T	Lime juice, freshly squeezed
¼ c	Soy sauce
⅓ c	Olive oil
½ c	Water

For tacos:

24	Mini corn tortillas (4-inch diameter)
1½ c	Finely chopped onion
1 c	Chopped fresh cilantro
12	Lime wedges
	Salsa or hot sauce, for serving, *optional*

s1 e9

Tester—Heather Huff

Marinate meat: In a large bowl or ziplock bag, combine all ingredients (keep meat in large pieces, don't cut). Cover or zip to close, then refrigerate overnight (minimum 4 hours).

Cook meat: Remove meat from refrigerator and discard marinade. Set meat on plate and bring to room temperature. Choose cooking method.

Grill: Heat outdoor barbeque grill, then place meat on hot grill. Grill for 4–5 minutes per side. The outside should be medium to dark brown and seared, but not burned. Remove from grill. Let rest 10 minutes.

Pan fry: Cut meat into strips about 5 inches long by 1 inch wide. Heat large skillet over high heat. Add 1 tablespoon butter. When butter is melted, move pan around so butter covers bottom as much as possible. Add strips of meat. Fry meat for 4–5 minutes per side. Remove strips and place them on a plate or cutting board. Let sit for 10 minutes.

Broil: If your broiler is in your oven, ensure oven rack is in top position. Turn on broiler. Cover a baking sheet with aluminum foil, shiny-side down. Arrange meat on baking sheet in a single layer with no overlapping. Place pan in broiler for 5–6 minutes. Remove pan, turn meat, then place pan back in broiler for another 5 minutes. Remove pan and let sit for 10 minutes.

Cut meat: Cut meat into small pieces, about ½ inch by ½ inch.

Heat tortillas: Stack the tortillas and wrap the stack in damp paper towels so tortillas are fully covered. Place tortillas in microwave oven. Cook on high for 2 minutes. When done, let tortillas sit in microwave for 1 minute. Remove from microwave and discard paper towels.

Assemble tacos: Place two tortillas on a flat work surface. Top with 1–2 tablespoons of meat, 1 teaspoon of onion, and 1 teaspoon of cilantro. Repeat for all tortillas. Serve with one lime wedge per taco and salsa or hot sauce.

Makes 12 street-style tacos.

GUACAMOLE

The horrible time when Rory and Lorelai were apart has ended. Rory has moved out of Richard and Emily's, is back in school, has gotten a job, and has returned home. To celebrate, she and Lorelai head to Luke's.

Lorelai is happy, relieved, and back to her quirky self. She has been going through all of the notes she wrote of topics she wanted to discuss with Rory once Rory returned. She finds one she cannot read and asks Luke if he remembers what the note says. He looks at it and notices it's written on the back of a receipt from a Mexican restaurant—a restaurant that charged six bucks for guacamole.

Luke's step-daughter just returned and he's just learned he has a long-lost daughter, but he's most focused on the six bucks he paid for guacamole. Sometimes Luke can be really annoying.

4	Avocadoes
½ c	Cored and chopped tomato
⅓ c	Peeled and minced onion
2 T	Minced cilantro
½	Jalapeño chile, stem removed
1 T	Olive oil
1½ T	Lemon juice, freshly squeezed
1 T	Kosher salt
½ t	Granulated garlic
¼ t	Black pepper
⅛ t	Cayenne pepper

Prepare avocadoes: Carefully cut each avocado in half, lengthwise. Remove and set aside pits. With a tablespoon, scoop out avocado into a medium mixing bowl.

Make guacamole: Add remaining ingredients to avocado. Using a large fork, begin mashing ingredients into avocado. Only mash a few times if you want chunky guacamole. Continue to mash more if you want a smoother consistency. (Guacamole may be eaten right away, but for full flavor, continue to next step.)

Chill guacamole: Press avocado pits into the top of the guacamole until they are submerged halfway. Cover bowl with plastic wrap. Refrigerate for 1 hour. Remove from refrigerator. Discard pits. Serve.

s6 e10

Tester—Devin Avellino

HOMEMADE TORTILLAS

TOWN FAVORITE

Richard runs a con on Rory, getting her to agree to visit Yale. In turn, Rory talks Lorelai into going, too. So, the senior Gilmores pick up Lorelai and Rory at home, then all four head to Yale. As they walk around campus, it's apparent they are having a fun day together—a rarity for this group. In an instant, the fun day ruptures when Richard tells Rory he's arranged for her to meet the Dean of Admissions. Rory takes the meeting but as soon as she emerges from the office, she and Lorelai take a cab back to Stars Hollow. Of course, on the way out of New Haven, they stop at Hector's Tacos—because Hector makes his own tortillas.

Corn Tortillas:

1½ c	Masa flour
1 c + 1 T	Water

Make dough: Pour flour into medium bowl. Add water. Mix with a fork until all flour has been moistened and a ball of dough forms. Remove dough from bowl and wrap in plastic wrap. Refrigerate 1 hour.

Press tortillas: Divide dough into 12 balls of equal size. If you have one, use a kitchen scale to get the size exact. Next, flatten each ball into a very thin, round tortilla. If you do not have a tortilla press, wrap two cutting boards in plastic wrap. Place one ball of dough on one of the cutting boards. Place the other cutting board on top and press down as hard as you can. Remove the tortilla to a plate and repeat for the remaining 11 balls.

Cook tortillas: In a small skillet or on a griddle, over medium-high heat, one by one, fry each tortilla for 45 seconds per side. Place each fried tortilla on a plate. Serve. Makes 12 tortillas.

Flour Tortillas:

3 c	Flour
1½ t	Baking powder
1 t	Salt
¼ c	Lard
1 c	Water

Make dough: In a large mixing bowl, combine flour, baking powder, and salt. Use a pastry cutter, a dough cutter, a large fork, or a knife to cut in the lard. Continue until the flour and lard look like tiny white peas. Add water slowly, in increments, and combine with a fork until a dough forms. Only use as much water as you need. If you need more than 1 cup of water, add 1 teaspoon at a time until dough sticks together well but isn't soupy. If you add too much water, add in more flour a tablespoon at a time until dough reaches the proper consistency. Wrap dough in plastic wrap and refrigerate for 1 hour.

Roll out tortillas: Separate dough into 24 balls of equal size. If you have one, use a kitchen scale to get the exact size. Cover a flat work surface with a light layer of flour. Place a ball of dough into the center of the flour and top it with a bit of flour. Using a rolling pin, roll out the dough into a thin circle, 6–7 inches in diameter. Repeat for all tortillas.

Cook tortillas: In a small skillet or on a griddle, over medium-high heat, one by one, fry each tortilla for 45 seconds per side. Place each fried tortilla on a plate. Cover with a clean towel. Once all tortillas have been cooked, serve. Makes 24 tortillas.

s3 e8

Tester—Melissa McAndrews

BEEF BURRITO
MADE WITH CHILE COLORADO

When the dinner at an exclusive restaurant Jason booked for his first date with Lorelai turns into a bust, the two head out in the car, searching for an alternate plan. From the road, Lorelai spots a Taco Barn, gets excited, and urgently directs Jason to pull into the drive-through. Lorelai places a massive order, including a beef burrito with no onions. When it's Jason's turn to order, he says he doesn't want anything, instantly killing Lorelai's excitement. This could have marked the end of a disastrous date. Instead, they pushed on until they found themselves at a grocery store, buying things to eat while also treating the trip like an errand, stocking up on personal items they each need. They had to work for it, but that night, outside, sitting at a metal picnic table, their fun, quirky relationship was born.

You'll have to work for this, too. These burritos require preparation of several elements. But, like Lorelai and Jason, if you push through, it'll all be worth it.

For refried beans:

½ lb (1 c)	Pinto beans, dried, washed
4 c	Water
¼ c	Cubed salt pork
1	Onion, peeled, *divided*
3 T	Oil (vegetable, canola, or safflower)

For Chile Colorado:

4 T	Butter, *divided*
2–3 lb	Beef chuck roast, trimmed, cubed
4 c	Water, *divided*
6–8	Dried New Mexico chiles (chiles Nuevo Mexico)*
1 T	Tequila
1 c	Peeled and finely chopped onion
3	Garlic cloves
1 t	Cornstarch
1½ t	Salt
1 t	Oregano, dried
2 t	Cumin

* may substitute 4 Pasilla negra chiles + 3-4 chiles de arbol

Slow cook beans: In a slow cooker, electric rice cooker, or Instant Pot, add beans, water, and salt pork. Cut onion in half. Quarter one of the halves and add to beans. Chop the remaining onion very finely and reserve for later. Cook beans on "high" for 2 hours. Skip down to the "brown meat" step to make the Chile Colorado while the beans are cooking.

Check beans for doneness: Once the beans have cooked for 2 hours, check for doneness. Use a spoon to remove 2–3 beans from the pot. Let them cool for a minute. Then taste them. If beans are still hard or partially hard, continue to cook. Check for doneness again every 15 minutes. When the beans feel soft and easy to bite into, they are done. Turn off heat. Beans may be served this way or fried to create refried beans (see next step).

Make refried beans: In a large skillet or Dutch oven, heat oil over medium-high heat. Add reserved chopped onion to hot oil. Sauté onions until translucent. Remove half of the beans from broth using a slotted spoon. Add beans to hot oil. Turn beans often. Use a potato masher to mash beans as you go. Continue to turn, mash, and fry beans for 5 minutes. (If you don't have a potato masher, pour the beans into a mixing bowl and use an electric mixer on low to medium-low speeds to mash the beans. Then return them to the pan to fry for 5–6 minutes.) Remove from heat and set aside.

Brown meat: In a large skillet or Dutch oven, melt 2 tablespoons butter over medium-high heat. Add meat. Use a wooden spoon or silicone spatula to move meat around until it browns on all sides. Add 2 cups of water. Cover. Continue to cook over low heat for 1 hour, stirring occasionally.

Prepare chiles: Boil the remaining 2 cups of water in a saucepan or a teakettle. Place chiles in a large, heat-proof bowl. Carefully pour water over chiles. Let them soak for 15–20 minutes. Once chiles are soft and malleable, take them out of the water and place them on a cutting board (reserve the water for later). Use a sharp knife to remove stems. Then slice chiles open along the side, fold open, and remove seeds.

Blend chiles: Place chiles in blender. Add 1 cup of soaking water plus ½ cup of broth from beef. Blend until smooth. Strain blended chiles into a bowl, through a sieve, pressing down on any solids to release liquids. Discard the solids. Mix the chiles into the beef. Add the remaining soaking water and the tequila to the beef. Stir to mix. Leave beef uncovered, cooking on medium-high heat for 10 minutes while the onions and garlic are cooking.

Sauté onions and garlic: In a separate skillet, melt butter over medium heat. Add onions and garlic. Cook until onion is translucent. Coat with cornstarch—consistency should feel like a paste.

Season beef: Add onion and garlic paste to beef. Stir to mix. Add salt, oregano, and cumin. Mix again. Cover. Reduce heat to low. Simmer for 90 minutes. Remove from heat. If chunks of meat are too large for burritos, pull the pieces apart using a fork.

Continued on the next page . . .

For rice:

2 T	Butter
1 c	Long-grain white rice
2½ c	Water
2	Roma tomatoes, cores removed, quartered
¾ c	Peeled and coarsely chopped onion, white or yellow
2	Garlic cloves, peeled
1	Large jalapeño chile, stem removed, quartered
1 T	Lemon or lime juice, freshly squeezed
1 t	Salt

For pico de gallo:

3	Roma tomatoes, cored, finely chopped
1 c	Peeled and finely chopped onion, red, white or yellow
1	Large jalapeño, stemmed, finely chopped
¼ c	Finely chopped cilantro
1 T	Lemon or lime juice, freshly squeezed
1 t	Salt
½ t	Black pepper

For burritos:

6	Flour tortillas, burrito-size, 12–14 inches in diameter
2 c	Shredded cheese, half Monterey Jack, half cheddar
2 c	washed, cored, and thinly sliced Iceberg lettuce
2 c	Guacamole (see recipe, page 71)
1 c	Sour cream or crema fresca
	Salsa and/or hot sauce for serving

Tester—Heather Huff

Eat Like a Gilmore DAILY CRAVINGS

Make rice: In a large saucepan, melt butter over medium heat. Add rice. Stir rice as it cooks—about 3 minutes. Add water. In a blender, add remaining ingredients and blend until pureed. Pour puree into rice. Bring rice to boil. Cover and reduce heat to low. Cook for 20–25 minutes. Remove from heat. Fluff with fork. Set aside.

Make pico de gallo: In a medium mixing bowl, combine all ingredients. Mix well. Cover and refrigerate until ready to use.

Heat tortillas: Wrap a stack of 6 tortillas in damp paper towels so tortillas are fully covered. Place tortillas in microwave oven. Cook on high for 90 seconds. When done, let tortillas sit in microwave for 1 minute. Remove from microwave and discard paper towels.

Assemble burritos: Lay one tortilla out on a flat surface. Place a scoop of beef (without broth) onto the tortilla about halfway between the center and the edge closest to you. Top the beef with a small scoop of beans, and then rice. Top the rice with cheese, then a little bit of pico de gallo, lettuce, guacamole, and sour cream. Feel free to make the burrito as small or as huge as you desire.

Fold the burrito: Lift the edge of tortilla closest to you over the top of the ingredients. Next, fold in the right edge, then left. Finally, place your hands around the burrito and roll it up, so it covers the top half of the tortilla. This is your burrito! Repeat for remaining tortillas. Serve with salsa or hot sauce.

Makes approximately 6 large burritos.

VALENTINE'S BURRITO

SOOKIE'S KITCHEN

Lorelai walks into the Dragonfly's kitchen to find Sookie despondent, on the verge of another bout of ennui. Sookie explains she has run out of creative food ideas and doesn't know what to serve for Valentine's Day. She's so desperate for a fresh idea that when Lorelai just pops out with the "burritos" idea, Sookie jumps on it. Lorelai eventually talks her out of making Valentine's Burritos for their guests. But what if Sookie had made them? What would they have had in them? How would they have tasted?

Like this, perhaps.

⅓ c	Parsley
3 T	Lemon Juice, freshly squeezed, *divided*
2 T	Olive oil, *divided*
2–3	Garlic cloves, peeled and minced
2	Chicken thighs, skinless, boneless, cubed
¾ lb	Chorizo sausage, ground or cut into ½-inch slices
12	Shrimp, shelled, deveined
1 c	Chicken broth, homemade or low-sodium packaged
½	Sweet yellow onion, medium
1	Jalapeño chile, stemmed, finely chopped
2	Roma tomatoes
½ t	Kosher salt
½ t	Black pepper
40	Saffron threads
¾ c	Arborio rice
½ c	Warm water
6	Flour tortillas, burrito-size
2 c	Shredded Monterey Jack cheese, *optional*
	Avocado, for serving
	Salsa and/or hot sauce, for serving, *optional*

Marinate chicken: In a medium bowl or a ziplock bag, combine parsley, 2 tablespoons of lemon juice, 1 tablespoon olive oil, and garlic. Add chicken thigh pieces to coat. Set aside, at room temperature.

Cook chorizo: Add ½ tablespoon olive oil to a deep frying pan or Dutch oven, over medium heat. Add chorizo. Cook for 4–5 minutes, stirring often. Use a slotted spoon to remove chorizo from pan and set aside. Reserve the oils in pan.

Cook chicken: In the same pan, add the chicken pieces (reserve the marinade) to the chorizo oils. Fry chicken for 2 minutes per side. Remove chicken from pan and set aside.

Cook shrimp: Add shrimp to same frying pan. Over medium heat, cook shrimp for 1 minute per side. Remove shrimp and set aside.

Warm broth: Add the broth to a medium saucepan and simmer over medium heat for 10 minutes.

Sauté vegetables: Using the same frying pan/Dutch oven, heat the remaining ½ tablespoon of olive oil over medium heat. Add the onion, pepper, and tomatoes. Sauté for 3 minutes. Remove from pan and set aside.

Make filling: Pour the lemon and garlic marinade mixture into frying pan/Dutch oven. Add salt, pepper, and saffron. Add rice. Stir until combined. Add the warm broth and water. Add meats. Cook, stirring every 2–3 minutes, until rice becomes al dente. Remove from heat. Let stand for 10 minutes.

Heat tortillas: Wrap a stack of 6 tortillas in damp paper towels so tortillas are fully covered. Place tortillas in microwave oven. Cook on high for 90 seconds. When done, let tortillas sit in microwave for 1 minute. Remove from microwave and discard paper towels.

Assemble burritos: Lay one tortilla out on a flat surface. Place a scoop of filling onto the tortilla about halfway between the center and the edge closest to you. Top the filling with a scoop of the cooked vegetables and some shredded cheese, if using. Feel free to make the burrito as small or as huge as you desire.

Fold the burrito: Lift the edge of the tortilla closest to you over the top of the ingredients. Next, fold in the right edge, then left. Finally, place your hands around the burrito and roll it up, so it covers the top half of the tortilla. This is your burrito! Repeat for remaining tortillas.

Serve: Serve with slices of avocado and your salsa or hot sauce of choice.

Tester—Liz Groff

Eat Like a Gilmore DAILY CRAVINGS

FIESTA BURGER

CONTRIBUTED BY KELLIE BEARD

Maybe it wasn't fair, the way Lorelai broke off her engagement to Max. Certainly, it was sudden. But it was the right thing to do. Max was a great guy—which Lorelai admits. He just wasn't for her. He couldn't keep up. He was too mild, too slow, too dull.

To illustrate this, take the night Max's car breaks down near Stars Hollow, which is also the first time he and Lorelai have a real date. They go to the Black, White, and Read movie theater and, to eat, Lorelai brings Fiesta Burgers from Al's. The burger is too hot for Max and he burns his tongue. Really? Come on, Max, keep up.

The Fiesta Burger is the perfect metaphor for Lorelai. She was too spicy for him—too quick, too creative, too spunky—and he got burned.

1	Avocado, halved, pitted
½ c	Peeled and finely chopped onion
½ c	Stemmed and finely chopped tomato
½ t	Salt
1	Lime, juiced
1 lb	Ground beef
2 T	Taco seasoning
2 t	Crushed red pepper
2	Jalapeños*, stemmed, sliced into rings
4	Slices pepper Jack cheese
	Sour cream, garnish
4	Burger buns
4	Lettuce leaves, chopped

Prepare guacamole topping: In a small bowl, mash together avocado, onion, tomato, and salt. Squeeze lime juice into mixture, stirring well. Set mixture aside.

Make patties: In a large bowl, combine ground beef with taco seasoning and crushed red pepper. Mix well. Form into four quarter-pound patties.

Cook patties: Place patties into a large skillet over medium-high heat. Cook burgers to desired doneness. Before removing patties from heat, place jalapeño rings on top of each patty, then top each with a slice of pepper Jack cheese. Remove burgers from heat once cheese has melted.

Assemble fiesta burgers: Spread sour cream on bottom of each bun. Place patties on buns and top with avocado mixture and chopped lettuce. Serve.

Substitute serrano chiles to add extra spice.

TAQUITOS
MADE WITH *CARNE DESHEBRADA* (shredded beef)

Sookie makes massive amounts of Lorelai's favorite foods and brings them over, all excited that Lorelai is going to tell her she's pregnant. Somehow, when Lorelai called and asked her to make food, all Sookie heard were the words "parents" and "expecting."

In reality, Lorelai was talking about Richard and Emily, her parents, that they were coming over, and she was expecting them soon.

While the taquitos and macaroni and cheese would have made the pefect "I'm pregnant" announcement food, it was completely inappropriate for the Gilmores.

To fix the problem, Sookie suggests calling the food names the Gilmores will recognize as more "high society" food—like calling the taquitos "blinis." It worked!

Whether you call these taquitos or blinis won't matter. Your guests will love them regardless of the name!

2 lb	Beef roast—tri tip, brisket, or chuck
1	Onion, white or yellow, peeled, coarsely chopped
2	Jalapeño peppers, stemmed, quartered
1	Serrano pepper, stemmed, quartered
5–6	Garlic cloves, peeled, smashed
½ c	Tequila
1 T	Kosher salt
30	Corn tortillas
	Oil for frying
	Salsa and guacamole for serving

Slow cook meat: Cut meat into 3–4 large chunks. In a slow cooker, Instant Pot, or electronic rice cooker, add meat, vegetables, garlic, tequila, and salt. Cook on high for 4 hours. Meat should come apart easily with a fork. Remove meat from pot, place in bowl. Discard all other contents of pot. Using two forks, shred the meat into fine strings of beef. Set aside.

Roll taquitos: Lay a tortilla on a flat work surface. Place pieces of shredded beef in a narrow row down the center of the tortilla. Roll tortilla into a thin tube, with beef in the center of it. Use a toothpick to hold the tortilla closed. Set the taquito on a plate, waiting to be fried. Repeat for all remaining tortillas.

Heat oil: In a large pot, Dutch oven, or deep skillet, add oil until it is 4 inches deep. Turn up to high heat and wait 10 minutes. Insert a wooden spoon into the oil. If small bubbles form around the spoon, your oil is ready to use. If not, wait a few more minutes then check again.

Prepare a drying station: Pile two paper towels on top of one another on a plate or cutting board. Place a drying rack on top of the paper towels. Place this drying station near the stove where you'll be frying, but far enough away that any flame from the burner won't come into contact with the paper towels.

Fry taquitos: Using tongs or a long, slotted spoon, carefully place 4–6 taquitos into the hot oil. Oil will pop, so take care to step back from the stove. Fry each taquito 1–2 minutes. Once a taquito is dark golden brown (not burned), remove it from the oil and place it on the drying rack. Repeat for all taquitos. Once taquitos have all been cooked, and cooled slightly, remove the toothpicks. Serve with salsa and/or guacamole.

Makes 30 taquitos.

Tester—Melissa McAndrews

MARGARITAS

YALE DAYS

With as much time as he was spending with Rory at the start of the new school year, Marty must have been feeling pretty good about the prospect of the two of them eventually dating. Then came that fateful day at the coffee cart when he introduced her to Logan. There was no hiding, either. Logan recognized his face instantly, even though it took him a moment to remember Marty's the guy who makes the great margaritas.

Marty's margaritas are legendary, even among heavy drinkers like Logan, Colin, and Finn. Now yours can be, too.

½ c   Sugar

½ c   Water

½ c   Lime juice, freshly squeezed

3 T   Orange juice, freshly squeezed

¼–½ c   Tequila

     Ice

     Coarse salt, for serving, *optional*

     Lime wedges, for garnish, *optional*

Make simple syrup: In a small saucepan, combine sugar and water. Heat over medium-high heat, stirring to blend. Once water begins to boil, remove from heat and let cool for 10 minutes.

Mix ingredients: In a blender (for blended) or pitcher (for on-the-rocks) combine lime juice, orange juice, and tequila. Stir in the simple syrup. Taste test. If you'd like stronger cocktails, add up to ¼ cup more tequila.

Prep glasses: Pour a generous amount of coarse salt onto a plate or shallow bowl. Moisten the outer rim of the glass(es) you'll be using. Place each glass, one at a time, upside down in the salt. Move the glass around until salt is sticking to the rim evenly on all sides. Repeat for all glasses.

Serve:

On-the-rocks: Fill each glass halfway with ice. Give margarita mixture one more thorough stir, then pour into each glass. Garnish with lime wedges. Serve.

Blended: In blender, add 2–3 cups of ice. Cover. Blend for 90 seconds. Look for margaritas to be frothy without any ice chunks. If there are chunks, blend for another 30 seconds. Pour into prepared glasses. Garnish with lime wedges.

Makes 3–4 margaritas.

s5e3

Tester—Shannon Huffman

HORS D'OEUVRES
& FINGER FOODS

LOBSTER PUFFS

A fabulous party at Richard and Emily Gilmore's with the most delicious lobster puffs. Cut to the headmasters office at Chilton—where a roaring fire and none other than Emily Gilmore await Lorelai and Rory for her first day. Lorelai's rodeo attire (thanks to a fuzzy blue clock) doesn't scream Hartford high-class lobster puffs. Yet when you make these you will remember that outfit.

While these lobster puffs may not get you any preferential treatment, they will bring a smile to your face. Not only will you remember the rodeo outfit and awkward encounter; you will remember the love and determination Lorelai and Emily shared for Rory and their desire to see her succeed in life.

1 pkg	Frozen puff pastry (Pepperidge Farm recommended)
2 T	Butter
2	Shallots, peeled, minced
1 T	Sherry
½ c	Mascarpone
1	Egg yolk
½ t	Salt
Pinch	Cayenne
Pinch	Ground nutmeg
¾ lb	Cooked, shelled, and chopped lobster
	Flour
1	Egg
¼ c	Water

Prepare pan(s) and oven: Set out 1 or 2 cookie sheets. Top each with parchment paper or a silicone mat. Set aside. Ensure oven racks are positioned toward center of oven. Preheat oven to 400°F.

Thaw puff pastry: Remove package from freezer. Let thaw at room temperature for 30 minutes.

Sauté shallots: In large saucepan, skillet, or Dutch oven, melt butter. Add shallots and sauté for 2–3 minutes, until shallots turn golden brown. Add sherry. Remove from heat and let cool for 15 minutes.

Make filling: In a large mixing bowl, combine mascarpone and egg yolk. Add salt, cayenne, and nutmeg. Mix. Add shallot mixture and lobster. Mix until fully combined.

Prepare puff pastry: On flat surface, sprinkle a thin layer of flour. Place one sheet of puff pastry on flour. Unfold and cut into three sections, following the natural crease in the dough. Cut each section into four equal rectangles.

Make egg wash: In a small bowl or ramekin, crack egg, add water, and mix with a fork until fully combined. Set aside.

Stuff and fold puffs: Along the long end of the rectangle, about ½ inch from edge, cut a ½-inch slit into each side (take care not to cut so far that it chops the whole end off). The little bit of dough on the short side of the slits will make the tail of your puff. Next, fold the tail. Pick up the corner nearest the slit you made and fold that corner over the short bit of dough, so the point extends over to the other side. Do the same for the other side. Then press down so the folded dough stays in place. Next, flip over the whole piece of dough. On the larger side of the slits/tail, place 2–3 teaspoons of lobster filling down the middle, starting at the "tail" end and going almost to the other end of the dough. Next, you're going to wrap the filling with pastry dough

(leaving the "tail" flat). Lift one side of the dough over the filling. Then lift the other side of the dough over the filling so it slightly overlaps the dough from the first side. Pinch the end opposite the "tail" so it's sealed. Use a sharp knife to gently cut several shallow slits across the top of the filled dough (to mimic a lobster shell). Place puff on pan and gently brush with egg wash. Repeat for all of the puff pastry.

Bake puffs: Place full trays in oven and bake for 15–17 minutes. Watch for the tops of the pastry to turn golden brown. Remove from oven, let cool for 2–3 minutes. Serve.

s1 e2   Intro by Fallon Hansen

Tester—Sarah Panizza

Eat Like a Gilmore DAILY CRAVINGS

MINI BAGEL DOGS

AT HOME

Mini bagel dogs combine two of Lorelai's favorite things—bagel dogs, which she likes to mow through four at a time, and mini hot dogs, which Sookie made for her when Richard and Emily were coming to visit. This way you can enjoy a bagel dog while still leaving room to eat that half bag of marshmallows.

9½ c + 2 T	Water, *divided*
4 T	Barley malt syrup, *divided*
1 pkg	Active dry yeast
4 c	High-gluten flour
2 t	Kosher salt
1	Egg
1 c	Shredded cheese, *optional* (cheddar or pepper Jack recommended)
25–30	Cocktail sausages (Lil Smokies recommended)
	Coarse sea salt
	Sauce(s) of choice for dipping

Bloom yeast: In a saucepan over medium heat, warm 1½ cups water to 110°F. Remove from heat. Stir in 2 tablespoons of barley malt syrup. Once combined, sprinkle the full package of yeast over the top. Let rest for 10 minutes. Watch for bubbling to occur and for a light foam to appear on top of the water. These indicate the yeast is ready to use. (After 15 minutes, if no bubbling has occurred, the yeast is likely ineffective. Discard the mixture and start again.)

Mix dough: In a large mixing bowl, mix together flour and salt. Pour in the yeast mixture. Using a hand mixer on lower speeds, mix together until a dough forms. Continue to mix the dough around the bowl for 3–5 minutes to activate the gluten. Remove the dough from bowl. Prepare a flat work surface by covering it with a light layer of flour. Then knead the dough for 20 minutes. Again, this will help to activate the gluten, which will give the bagels the chewy exterior we all love!

Prepare the dough: Lightly grease the inside of a large bowl. Set dough into bowl and cover with a clean kitchen towel. Let dough rise for 1 hour. After an hour, the dough should have doubled in size. Next, punch down the dough, which sounds rough, but isn't. Please continue to be gentle with your dough! Push into the center of the dough until it is deflated. Then pull the edges away from the bowl and toward the center of the dough. Prepare a lightly floured work surface again. Take the dough out of the bowl and place it on the floured surface. Gently knead the dough for 10 turns. Form dough into a ball and let it rest on the work surface. Cover the dough with the kitchen towel, plastic wrap, or an inverted bowl to keep it from drying out. Wait 10 minutes. Your dough is now ready to use!

Prepare pan(s) and oven: Take out 1 or 2 cookie sheets. Cover each with parchment paper or a silicone baking mat. If using neither paper nor mat, lightly grease the bottom of each pan with butter or oil. Set aside. Ensure oven racks are set to the center of the oven (not the top or bottom positions). Preheat oven to 425°F.

Prepare for boiling: Pour 8 cups of water into a stockpot or Dutch oven. Add the remaining 2 tablespoons of barley malt syrup. Heat on high until boiling. While waiting for it to boil, move on to the next two steps.

Make egg wash: In a ramekin or small bowl, combine 2 tablespoons water plus the egg. Use a fork to combine.

Wrap sausages: Divide dough into four equal pieces. Working with one piece at a time, on a floured work surface, roll out the dough using a rolling pin. Roll dough into a long, thin strip roughly 2 inches wide by 12–14 inches long. Use a knife, dough cutter, or pizza wheel to cut dough into 2 inch x 2 inch squares. If using cheese, top each square with 1–2 teaspoons of cheese. Place mini sausage on the square diagonally. Starting at one side corner, wrap the dough around the sausage while slowly rolling the sausage to the other side. Fold over the ends of the dough to cover the ends of the sausage. Brush egg wash on the seams to secure. Set aside. Repeat until all sausages have been wrapped.

Boil mini bagel dogs: Stack two paper towels on a plate, then place a drying rack on the paper towels. This is where you'll place the mini bagel dogs after they boil. Use a slotted spoon to lower 4–6 mini dogs at a time into the boiling water. Allow them to boil for 2 minutes. Then remove them onto the drying rack. Repeat for all.

Bake mini bagel dogs: Transfer each bagel dog to a prepared cookie sheet. Top each one with a pinch of coarse sea salt. Place cookie sheets in oven and bake for 15 minutes. Bagel dogs will be done when their tops are golden brown. Remove from oven. Let cool.

Serve: Serve right away with dipping sauce(s) of choice.

Tester—Gabi Faber

Eat Like a Gilmore DAILY CRAVINGS

HOMEMADE TATER TOTS

Lorelai and Rory do more with Tater Tots than anyone in the history of Tater Tots. Now you can, too. Top your pizza with tots. Fill your taco with tots. Or top your tots with chili and cheese. They're an appetizer, a main course, and a topping, all wrapped in a neat tot package.

6	Medium potatoes, peeled (Yukon Gold recommended)
8–10 c	Water
2 t	Salt
1 t	Black pepper
2 T	Cornstarch
1 Qt	Oil (vegetable, canola, or safflower)

Parboil potatoes: Place peeled potatoes in large saucepan or Dutch oven. Fill pot with water just until potatoes are covered. Bring water to a boil over high heat. Boil for 3–4 minutes. Remove from heat. Pour out water. Allow potatoes to sit in pan until they are cool enough to handle.

Grate potatoes: If you have a food processor, cut potatoes into smaller chunks and work in batches, grating the potatoes in the food processor. If you do not have a food processor, grate the potatoes on a box grater. (If your grater has the option for a fine grate, use that one.) Place grated potatoes in large bowl.

Make tots: Add salt, pepper, and cornstarch to potatoes. Mix well, using your hands. Form potatoes into tots by rolling a small ball of potato mixture between your palms. Then use your fingers to mold the ball into a cylinder. Repeat until all of the potato mixture has been formed into tots.

Prepare drying rack: Near the stove, on a flat work surface or large cutting board, stack two paper towels. Top the paper towels with a cooling rack.

Fry tots: In a deep fryer, stockpot, or Dutch oven, heat oil to 350–360°F. Fry tots in batches—about 6–8 tots at a time. When tots are a medium golden brown on all sides, remove from oil using tongs or a slotted spoon. Place on drying rack. While tots are still a bit oily, add salt as desired. Repeat for all remaining tots. Serve with ketchup or dipping sauce of choice.

Makes about 40 tots.

Tester—Liz Groff

ONION RINGS

Sometimes Luke is so busy taking care of everyone else's needs, he neglects his own needs. When Jess moves in and crowds their apartment, Luke takes to watching a tiny TV downstairs in the dark, empty diner, which smells like onion rings. Fortunately, Lorelai looks out for him by encouraging him to hunt for a bigger apartment.

Don't let the thought of the onion rings' smell deter you, though. The lovely crunch and flavor make it all worthwhile!

2	Sweet onions, peeled, sliced
2 c	Buttermilk
1½ c	Flour
½ c	Cornstarch
2 c	Bread crumbs, panko recommended
1 T	Paprika
1 T	Black pepper
1 t	Cayenne
1 qt	Oil, for frying
1–3 T	Salt
	Ranch dressing, for serving, *optional*

Soak onions: Separate onion slices into rings and place them in a large ziplock bag. Add buttermilk. Refrigerate for 1 hour.

Dredge onions: In one large, shallow bowl, combine flour and cornstarch. Remove onions from buttermilk, reserving buttermilk. Place 2–3 onion rings in flour/cornstarch and coat on both sides. Place coated onions on a large plate or cutting board.

Batter and coat onions: Add buttermilk to flour/cornstarch and whisk together. In a second large, shallow bowl, combine bread crumbs, paprika, pepper, and cayenne. Mix using a fork until fully combined. Place each onion ring in the buttermilk batter, coating on both sides. Place battered onion in spiced bread crumbs. Coat on both sides. Place onion ring on a clean, large plate or cutting board. Repeat for all onion rings.

Heat oil: Pour oil into stockpot or Dutch oven. Place a candy thermometer in pot. Over medium-high heat, heat oil to 350–360°F.

Prepare drying rack: Near the stove, on a flat work surface or large cutting board, stack two paper towels. Top the paper towels with a cooling rack.

Fry onion rings: Carefully place 4–6 onion rings in oil. Fry until golden brown, then flip each ring. Again, fry until golden brown. Total fry time will be 1–2 minutes. Remove rings from oil using tongs or long fork. Place fried rings on drying rack. Repeat for all rings. Sprinkle rings with salt to taste. Serve with ranch dressing, if using.

Makes approximately 40 onion rings.

FRENCH DIP SLIDERS

FESTIVAL FOOD

When weather traps Taylor at his sister's house, he calls an emergency town meeting at 3 a.m. He's worried the Winter Carnival will suffer in his absence, causing folks to miss out on all their favorite festival treats, like French dips. With all the attendees in their pajamas, they decide Kirk will take over for Taylor. Problem solved. Everyone goes back to bed to dream about the festival and their French dip sandwiches.

4 T	Butter, *divided*
3 c	Peeled and thinly sliced sweet onion
2 t	Fresh minced thyme
1 T	Peeled and minced garlic
¼ c	Sherry, *divided*
¼ t	Sugar
2 c	Beef broth
1 T	Worcestershire sauce
1	Beef bouillon cube
½ t	Kosher salt
12	Slider buns, Parker House–style dinner rolls, or Hawaiian rolls
½ lb	Swiss cheese, thinly sliced
1 lb	Roast beef, deli style, thinly sliced

Caramelize onions: In a large frying pan or Dutch oven, melt 2 tablespoons butter over medium-high heat. Add onions. If onions are in round slices, separate each circle into separate rings as it drops into pan. Sauté onions for 5–6 minutes until soft. Add thyme, garlic, and half of the sherry. Continue to sauté, stirring occasionally, until all sherry has been absorbed. Sprinkle with sugar, then add remaining sherry. Sauté until most of the sherry has been absorbed.

Make jus: Add beef broth, Worcestershire sauce, beef bouillon cube, and kosher salt to onions. Stir until combined. Reduce heat to low and simmer, uncovered, for 15 minutes.

Prepare pan and oven: Set out a baking sheet covered with parchment paper or a silicone baking mat. Set aside. Ensure oven rack is in the center position. Preheat oven to 350°F.

Assemble sliders: Using a serrated knife, carefully cut buns/rolls into top and bottom buns. Place bottom rolls on the pan, with all of them side by side, touching. Layer the entire bun surface with slices of Swiss cheese, until it's all evenly covered in cheese 1–2 slices deep. Do the same with roast beef, only make the meat thicker. Place any extra cheese in another layer on top of the beef. Use a large fork or slotted spoon to pull onions out of the jus. Cover the surface of the cheese/beef with a generous layer of onions. Use all of the onions! Place a top bun on each slider.

Bake sliders: Melt the remaining 2 tablespoons of butter. Lightly brush butter onto tops of buns. Place pan in oven for 10–12 minutes, just long enough to heat the roast beef and melt the cheese.

Serve sliders: Once cheese is melted, remove pan from oven. Using a large, sharp knife, carefully cut the sliders into individual sandwiches. Serve with remaining jus on the side for dipping.

s6e12

SOFT PRETZEL GOAT CHEESE BITES

We all want to see this modern feat of Sookie's—the pretzel basket stuffed with goat cheese. But how does one serve a basket? These little bites take out the "basket" part, leaving just the pretzel stuffed with goat cheese. All the flavor without the awkward basket shape.

1½ c	Water
1 pkg	Active dry yeast
2 t	Sugar
4 c	High-gluten flour
2 t	Kosher salt
6 c	Water
½ c	Baking soda
1	Egg
3 T	Butter
4 oz	Goat Cheese

Bloom yeast: In a medium saucepan, warm water to 110°F only (no hotter). Sprinkle the full package of yeast onto water. Then sprinkle sugar onto yeast. Watch for bubbling to occur and for a light foam to appear on top of the water. These indicate the yeast is ready to use. (After 15 minutes, if no bubbling has occurred, the yeast is likely ineffective. Discard the mixture and start again.)

Mix dough: In a large mixing bowl, mix together flour and salt. Pour in the yeast mixture. Using a hand mixer on lower speeds, mix together until a dough forms. Continue to mix the dough around the bowl for 3–5 minutes to activate the gluten. Remove the dough from bowl. Prepare a flat work surface by covering it with a light layer of flour. Then knead the dough for 20 minutes. Again, this will help to activate the gluten.

Prepare the dough: Lightly grease the inside of a large bowl. Set dough into bowl and cover with a clean kitchen towel. Let dough rise for 1 hour. After an hour the dough should have doubled in size. Next, punch down the dough, which sounds rough, but isn't. Please continue to be gentle with your dough! Push into the center of the dough until it is deflated. Then pull the edges away from the bowl and toward the center of the dough. Prepare a lightly floured work surface again. Take the dough out of the bowl and place it on the floured surface. Gently knead the dough for 10 turns. Form dough into a ball and let it rest on the work surface. Cover the dough with the kitchen towel, plastic wrap, or an inverted bowl to keep it from drying out. Wait 10 minutes. Your dough is now ready to use!

Prepare pan(s) and oven: Take out 1 or 2 cookie sheets. Cover each with parchment paper or a silicone baking mat. If using neither paper nor mat, lightly grease the bottom of each pan with butter or oil. Set aside. Ensure oven racks are set to the center of the oven (not the top or bottom positions). Preheat oven to 450°F.

Prepare for boiling: Pour 6 cups of water into a stockpot or Dutch oven. Add the baking soda. Heat on high until boiling. While waiting for it to boil, move on to the next two steps.

Make egg wash: In a ramekin or small bowl, combine 2 tablespoons water plus the egg. Use a fork to combine.

Make pretzel bites: Divide dough into four equal pieces. Working with one piece at a time on a floured work surface, roll out the dough using a rolling pin. Roll dough into a long, thin strip—roughly 2 inches wide by 12–14 inches long. Carefully spread a quarter of the cheese onto the dough, keeping it away from the edges. Brush egg wash onto the top edge. Roll the bottom edge up to cover the cheese. Roll the top edge down until it overlaps the bottom edge by a quarter inch. Gently press the seam to make sure it is secure. Use a knife, dough cutter, or pizza wheel to cut dough into 2-inch pieces. Crimp together the ends of each piece using a fork or your fingers. Set each piece on a plate or cutting board. Repeat until all pieces have been stuffed. Cover pieces with a towel and allow them to rise again for 30 minutes.

Boil pretzel bites: Stack two paper towels on a plate, then place a drying rack on the paper towels. This is where you'll place the pretzel bites after they boil. Use a slotted spoon to lower 4–6 pieces at a time into the boiling water. Allow them to boil for 2 minutes. Then remove them onto the drying rack. Repeat for all.

Bake pretzel bites: Transfer each piece to a prepared cookie sheet. Brush the top of each one with a thin coat of melted butter. Place cookie sheets in oven and bake for 15 minutes. Pretzel bites will be done when their tops are golden brown. Remove from oven. Let cool.

Serve: Serve right away with dipping mustard of choice.

Tester—Melissa McAndrews

Eat Like a Gilmore DAILY CRAVINGS

KIMCHI DUMPLINGS

MRS KIM'S

After she and Zach break up, Lane moves home. Lane's angry, miserable, and difficult to live with. Mrs. Kim makes these dumplings in an attempt to lift Lane's spirits. But it's actual spirits—two tiny sips of alcohol—plus a rare expression of compassion from Mrs. Kim that finally snap Lane out of it.

For dumplings:

1½ c	Strained and coarsely chopped kimchi
8 oz.	Firm or extra firm tofu block, liquid removed
½ c	Peeled and finely chopped shallots
¼ c	Finely chopped green onions, white parts
1 T	Peeled and minced garlic
2 t	Peeled and finely chopped fresh ginger
2 T	Soy sauce
2 t	Sesame oil, toasted
½ t	Salt
¼ t	Black pepper
¼ t	White pepper
2 T	Water
30	Round pot sticker/dumpling wrappers
	Oil, for frying

For sauce:

¼ c	Soy sauce
¼ c	Kimchi liquid (reserved from dumplings)
2 T	Sugar
½ t	Crushed red pepper flakes

Mix vegetables and tofu: In large mixing bowl, combine kimchi, tofu, shallots, green onions, garlic, and ginger. Add soy sauce, sesame oil, salt, and peppers. Mix thoroughly. This is your filling.

Stuff dumplings: Lightly flour a large plate, flat pan, or cutting board. Set aside. Place one dumpling wrapper on a flat work surface. Spoon 2 teaspoons of filling into middle of wrapper. Dip finger in the 2 tablespoons of water, then run it around the outer edge of wrapper to moisten. Fold wrapper so edges meet up. Fold the edge into 5–6 pleats. Set dumpling on floured plate. Repeat until all filling has been used.

Prepare drying rack: Place two paper towels on a plate or cutting board. Top the paper towels with a cooling rack.

Heat oil: Fill a deep skillet or Dutch oven with ¼ inch of oil. Over medium-high heat, bring oil temperature to 330–340°F. If you don't have a thermometer, check temperature by carefully placing a small, torn bit of dumpling wrapper into oil. When it sizzles, the oil is ready.

Fry dumplings: Carefully add dumplings in a single layer (not all dumplings will fit; make multiple batches). Fry until golden brown on bottom. Flip dumplings. Fry until a light layer of golden brown crust appears on the bottom of dumplings. Remove dumplings from pan. Repeat for additional batches, if needed.

Make sauce: In a small bowl, combine all ingredients. Stir to combine.

Serve: Serve dumplings with sauce.

Makes 30 dumplings.

s6e11

SALTY NUTS WITH LEMONADE

Yes, Taylor blew the entire Spring Fling budget on the hay bale maze, leaving Gypsy without her lemonade booth and Morey without his salty nuts booth. Fortunately, Sookie was able to step in and make both, so the poor families who waited all winter for those springtime favorites wouldn't be disappointed. Plus, they got to enjoy the maze. It was a win-win for them.

For us, it wasn't. We still had to sit at home dreaming about the lemonade and the salty nuts. Until now!

For nuts:

5 c	Roasted, unsalted mixed nuts
5 T	Butter, melted
1 T	Kosher salt

Prepare pan and oven: Place a piece of parchment paper on a baking sheet. Ensure oven rack is in center position. Preheat oven to 170°F.

Prepare nuts: Place nuts in a one-gallon ziplock plastic bag. Add melted butter and salt. Zip the bag closed and gently shake and massage nuts until butter and salt are evenly distributed.

Bake nuts: Empty the nuts out onto the pan, spreading them out as much as possible. Bake for 90 minutes. Remove from oven. Add additional salt, if desired. Serve.

Makes 5 cups.

For lemonade:

2 c	Sugar
2 c	Water
3 c	Lemon juice, freshly squeezed
6 c	Water
	Ice
	Mint leaves, garnish

Make simple syrup: In a medium saucepan, combine sugar with water. Over medium heat, stir until the sugar is fully dissolved. Remove from heat.

Make lemonade: In a large pitcher or beverage dispenser, combine simple syrup, lemon juice, and water. Stir to combine.

Serve lemonade: Add ice to lemonade or add ice to glasses then pour lemonade into glasses. Garnish with mint leaves. Serve.

Makes 12 cups.

CALIFORNIA ROLL SUSHI

To help Lorelai turn her home into Asia for Rory, Sookie gives her a crash course in sushi-making. Before Lorelai derails the class with talk of fried chicken sushi, meatloaf sushi, and the infamous dessert sushi, Sookie shows her how to make the traditional california roll. A classic!

For rice:

1½ c	Medium-grain rice
2 c	Water
2 T	Sushi-seasoned rice vinegar

For sushi roll:

4 sheets	Seaweed paper/Nori
½ c	Sesame seeds, toasted
1	Avocado, halved, pitted, peeled, sliced into ⅛-inch pieces
1	Cucumber (Persian, English, or Japanese), peeled, seeded,* cut into thin strips
4	Crab meat or imitation crab/surimi, separated into thin pieces
	Soy sauce
	Wasabi
	Pickled ginger

* if using Japanese cucumber, there will be no seeds to remove

Rinse rice: Place rice in a bowl or pan and cover with water. Using your hands, rinse the rice in the water for a couple of minutes, until water is very murky. Strain rice. Repeat until water no long becomes murky. Strain rice thoroughly to remove all excess water.

Cook rice: Place rice in a saucepan which has a tight-fitting lid, or in a rice maker. Add 2 cups water and the vinegar.

If using a pan—bring water to a boil over medium-high heat. Once water begins boiling, reduce heat to low and cover pot with lid. Let cook for 20 minutes. Check for doneness after 15 minutes. Lift lid and check for liquid remaining in pan. If you see liquid or hear it bubbling below the surface of the rice, replace lid and cook for an additional 5 minutes. If all liquid has been absorbed, remove from heat.

If using a rice cooker—cook rice using the "White Rice" setting.

Cool rice: Once rice is fully cooked, scoop rice into shallow bowl, plate, or baking dish, allowing it to cool to room temperature prior to making sushi.

Make roll: On a flat work surface, place one piece of seaweed paper, shiny-side down. Cover the paper with rice, about ¼-inch thick. Leave ¼ inch of space empty at the bottom. Sprinkle the rice with sesame seeds, as desired. Turn seaweed over. Along the bottom third, assemble a few avocado slices, cucumber pieces, and crab pieces in a line all the way across the seaweed paper.

Roll sushi: Begin rolling the sushi from the bottom, keeping the roll as intact and tight as possible. Roll into a long, tight tube. Cut the tube into 6–8 round pieces. Arrange on a plate. Serve with soy sauce, wasabi, and pickled ginger.

Tester— Shannon Huffman

MINI ORANGE BISCUITS
WITH HONEY-MUSTARD HAM & CHEDDAR

For Rory's sixteenth birthday party (the normal party at Lorelai's house, not the stuffy, high-society party Emily throws), Sookie jumps in and helps Lorelai make food. This is one of the things she makes—tiny ham sandwiches on tiny orange biscuits. This episode takes place very early on in the series, at a point when we're still getting to know the characters. The first time we hear Sookie describe this dish, she captures our attention and helps us understand how truly talented she is.

For ham:

1	Ham, 3–5 pounds (if ham is larger, double the amount of mustard, honey, and cloves)
½ c	Mustard of choice, plus more for serving
1 c	Honey
1 t	Ground cloves

For biscuits:

2½ c	Flour
3 t	Baking powder
1 t	Baking soda
¾ c + 1 T	Butter, cold
1 T	Honey
1 c	Orange juice, freshly squeezed
3 T	Orange zest
18	Slices cheddar cheese, for assembly

Prepare oven: Place rack in lowest or second to lowest position. Preheat oven to 350°F.

Prepare ham: Cover a roasting pan or large baking dish in two long sheets of aluminum foil. Place ham cut-side down on pan. In a large measuring cup, mix together mustard, honey, and cloves. Brush or spoon one half of the mixture onto the top of the ham, distributing evenly. Pull up sides of foil to cover ham fully. Through the foil, insert meat thermometer into ham.

Bake ham: Place ham in oven. Bake until thermometer reads 140°F. This will take about 15 minutes per pound of ham. Remove ham from oven. Increase oven temperature to 450°F. Remove foil from top of ham. Brush remaining honey mustard mixture onto top of ham, distributing evenly. Place ham back in oven. Bake for 10–15 minutes. Watch for outside of ham to turn very brown, but not burn. Remove from oven. Let rest for 30 minutes.

Prepare pan for biscuits: Set out 1 or 2 cookie sheets. Cover with parchment paper or silicone baking mats. Set aside. Keep oven set to 450°F but move rack to center position.

Make biscuits: In large mixing bowl, combine flour, baking powder, and baking soda. Using a pastry cutter, dough cutter, or knife, cut in butter until flour looks like coarse little pebbles. Add honey, orange juice, and orange zest. Mix with a fork, only until combined and a dough forms.

Knead and cut biscuits: Cover a flat work surface with a light layer of flour. Turn dough out onto flour and knead by hand for 8–10 turns. Cover a rolling pin in a light layer of flour. Roll dough out until it is about ½ inch thick. Use a 1½-inch dough cutter. If you don't have a cutter, find a small glass, a shot glass, a small jar, or a clean bottle cap to cut dough into 1½ inch circles. Place each circle onto prepared pan. Reroll and cut dough until all dough has been used. Brush biscuits with melted butter. Place pan in oven. Bake for 8 minutes. Remove and let cool for 10 minutes.

Slice ham: Place ham on its side, on a cutting board. Slice ham in ⅛th inch slices. Cut slices into 6 dozen 2-inch squares. Set aside. Slice remaining ham, wrap, and store.

Cut cheese: Cut each slice of cheese in a crisscross—one cut down center, one cut across middle—to form 4 small squares per slice. Set aside.

Assemble mini sandwiches: Cut a biscuit horizontally across middle to create a top half and bottom half. Place a drop of mustard on the bottom half, then add two squares of ham plus one square of cheese. Place top half of biscuit on top. Secure with toothpick, if desired. Repeat for all biscuits. Serve.

Makes 36 mini sandwiches.

Tester—Jamie Francis

Eat Like a Gilmore DAILY CRAVINGS

Meats, Seafood & Main Dishes

CHICKEN PICCATA

TOWN FAVORITE

To say that we all love Dave Rygalski is an understatement, right? The guy clearly loves Lane, shares her deep interest in music (and subterfuge), and goes out of his way to win over Mrs. Kim. He's just lovely.

Lane must have been so excited to get to go to prom with Dave. Well, we know she was excited, because she handed Rory a giant shopping bag filled with the photos she took that night. Pretend this is photo number one—their chicken piccata.

1 lb	Chicken breast filets, boneless, skinless
1½ c	Flour
1 t	Salt
1 t	Pepper
1 T	Butter
1 T	Olive oil
4	Garlic cloves, peeled, smashed
¾ c	Vermouth
½ c	Lemon juice
1 T	Capers
1 T	Minced Italian parsley
1	Lemon, sliced, garnish
	Cooked angel-hair pasta, for serving

Prepare chicken: If chicken fillets are more than ¾ inch thick, use a meat mallet to pound them down to ¾ inch thickness. In a shallow bowl, combine flour, salt, and pepper. Dredge chicken pieces in flour mixture, so both sides of each fillet are coated. Place chicken on plate and set aside.

Heat oils and garlic: In a wide frying pan, melt butter over medium-high heat. Add olive oil. Swirl together. Sauté garlic until fragrant, about 1 minute. Remove garlic cloves and discard.

Cook chicken: Add chicken fillets to oil, arranging them in a single layer, close together. Cook each side 3–4 minutes, until chicken turns white, but not browned. Keep heat on but remove fillets from pan. Place them on a clean plate and set aside.

Make sauce: Add vermouth to pan and deglaze. Add lemon juice, capers, and parsley. Stir together. Heat for 1 minute. Remove from heat.

Serve: Arrange chicken pieces on a serving platter or bed of angel-hair pasta. Pour sauce over chicken. Garnish with lemon slices. Serve.

Makes 3–4 servings.

s3e22 **Tester**—Sarah Lea Phelps

OSSO BUCO

CONTRIBUTED BY BRIAN ANDERSON

Lorelai is too quick for Max, example #2: Max tells Lorelai an elaborate story about some old woman who taught him to make osso buco. Lorelai sees right through the lie while he's still telling it.

In truth, it doesn't matter who teaches you to make osso buco. Just make the osso buco.

3	Bacon slices
2 T	Extra-virgin olive oil
1 c	Flour, *divided*
1½ lb	Country-style boneless pork ribs
	Salt, to taste
	Freshly ground black pepper, to taste
1	Red onion, diced
4	Carrots, peeled, cut into ⅛-inch coins
2	Celery stalks, diced
2	Garlic cloves, peeled, chopped
1 c	Dry white wine
1 T	Tomato paste
2	Roma tomatoes, diced
2 t	Chopped fresh rosemary, (may substitute 1 t dry rosemary)
1 t	Chopped fresh sage (may substitute ½ t dry sage)
Pinch	Crushed red pepper
3½ c	Chicken broth (chicken bone broth recommended)
1 T	Worcestershire sauce
1	Beef soupbone (usually available from butcher)
1 T	Butter
	Cooked white rice, for serving, *optional*

Note: This dish is traditionally made with veal shanks. They can be hard to find, expensive, and have some sinewy, slimy textures you have to eat around. So I'm using country-style pork ribs instead—adding in a soupbone for the marrow that melts into the sauce. The dish turns out almost exactly the same and delicious.

Fry bacon: Over medium-high heat, fry the bacon in a stockpot or Dutch oven. Use tongs or a fork to remove and place on a paper towel. Leave the fat in the pot and add 2 tablespoons of extra-virgin olive oil.

Brown pork rib(s): Place the flour in a shallow, wide bowl or on a plate. (Reserve 1 tablespoon of flour to use later.) Pat the ribs dry and season with salt and pepper. Dredge each piece of pork in the flour, then immediately place in pot. Brown all pieces on both sides. (If you are making a larger batch, only brown 3 pieces at a time so you don't crowd the pot.) Brown is important . . . black is burnt and not good. Watch the heat—keep it set to medium-high. Remove the pork, place it on a plate, tent the plate with aluminum foil, and set aside.

Sauté vegetables: Lower the heat to medium. Using the same pot, add the onion, carrots, and celery. Season with a little salt and pepper. Sauté until soft and the onions are translucent, about 8 minutes. Add the garlic and sauté 1 more minute.

Make sauce: Add the white wine, then turn the heat back to medium-high. Gently boil the wine while stirring and scraping up the brown bits from the bottom of the pot with a wooden spoon. Continue until the wine is reduced by half, about 5 minutes. Add the tomato paste and stir to combine. Add the tomatoes, rosemary, and sage and stir in. Add the chicken broth. Add the Worcestershire sauce. Add the pinch of crushed red pepper and stir to combine.

Simmer: Return the pork to the pot along with the soupbone. Bring to a boil, then cover the pot. Reduce heat to low and simmer about 1½ hours until the meat is fork-tender. Open and stir every 20 minutes. Adjust liquid with water if necessary (liquid should just cover the meat).

For the gremolata:

3 T	**Chopped fresh parsley**
1 T	**Lemon zest**
2 T	**Chopped chives or green onions (green parts)**
2 T	**Extra-virgin olive oil**

Make the gremolata: In a small bowl, combine the parsley, lemon zest, and chives with the extra-virgin olive oil and a little salt and pepper and stir together. Set aside.

Thicken sauce: Combine a tablespoon of butter and a tablespoon of flour in a small bowl and mush the two into a paste. Remove the meat to a serving platter. Whisk the paste in the pot and turn up heat to high until sauce is at a boil. Gently boil until the sauce is thick and luscious, about 5 minutes. Check if it needs a little more salt, then add salt to taste.

Serve: Pour the sauce over the meat. Spoon the gremolata all around the top and crumble up the bacon and sprinkle on top as well. Serve over plain white rice. Boom!

s1 e11

ROASTED TURKEY LEGS

FESTIVAL FOOD

During the short window of time Liz and TJ have to plan their wedding in the town square, their turkey legs guy gets arrested for violating his parole. This means Luke has to step in and come to their rescue, again. Even after Liz specifically promised him he wouldn't have to do anything.

What's worse, while he's making the turkey legs, Liz's girlfriends are mocking him. Don't get roped into making these turkey legs. Only make them if you want to make them.

4	Turkey drumsticks
1 T	Kosher salt
1 T	Ground black pepper
1 T	Granulated garlic
1 T	Paprika (not smoked)
1 T	Dried thyme
¼ c	Butter, melted

Prepare pan and oven: Use a roasting pan or baking sheet (with sides). Cover with aluminum foil, shiny-side down. Ensure oven rack is in center position. Preheat oven to 375°F.

Prepare turkey legs: Rinse turkey legs and pat dry with paper towels. Stand each leg up and carefully run a knife down each leg 2 or 3 times, making little crevices.

Rub legs: In a small bowl, combine salt, pepper, garlic, paprika, and thyme. Rub each leg generously with spice mix, getting extra rub into the crevices.

Roast legs: Place legs on pan. Brush with melted butter on all sides. Place pan in oven. Roast for 90 minutes, turning once at the 45-minute mark. Insert a meat thermometer. Meat is done when it reaches 180°F. Remove from oven. Let stand 10 minutes. Serve.

s4e21

BREADED FRENCH COUNTRY CHICKEN

Luke and Lorelai eat very differently. Granted, Luke can get a little pushy with his views, sneaking baked chips and decaf coffee to Lorelai when he serves her. Overall, though, he lets her eat the way she wants without much commentary.

When Lorelai and Rory have a movie night and Luke comes to work on his boat, he even tells Lorelai he doesn't want to know what food she's preparing. Lorelai jokingly fibs, telling him she's preparing breaded French country chicken.

Lorelai may have been joking, but this chicken is amazing. It's probably not movie night material, but it'll definitely work for a Friday night dinner.

4	Chicken breasts, boneless, skinless
1	Egg, beaten
1 c	Bread crumbs
1 T	Herbs de Provence
2 t	Salt
2 t	Black pepper
3 T	Butter
4	slices Muenster cheese
	Parsley or thyme, for garnish

Prepare chicken: Wash chicken and pat dry with paper towels. Place beaten egg in a medium, shallow bowl. In a second shallow bowl, combine bread crumbs, Herbs de Provence, salt, and pepper. Dip one breast in egg, covering both sides. Hold breast over bowl and allow excess egg to drip off. Dredge breast through bread crumbs until covered on both sides. Place breast on a plate or clean cutting board. Repeat for remaining 3 breasts.

Cook chicken: In a large frying pan or Dutch oven, melt butter over medium heat. Distribute melted butter so bottom of pan is covered. Place breaded breasts in pan. Cook breasts for 5 minutes. Turn breasts. Cook for 3 minutes. Place a piece of cheese on top of each breast. Remove from heat. Allow chicken to rest in pan for 10 minutes. Place chicken on plates and garnish with parsley or fresh thyme.

Makes 4 servings.

Tester— Jamie Francis

Eat Like a Gilmore DAILY CRAVINGS

LOBSTER BISQUE

SOOKIE'S KITCHEN

Lobster bisque is one of the few dishes we know for a fact Sookie made regularly, both at the Independence Inn, and later at the Dragonfly. We first learn of it early in season 1, when Lorelai reads aloud the rave review from the restaurant critic. Then, toward the end of season 7, when Michel brings PawPaw into the Inn, Sookie mentions not wanting any dog hair to get into the guests' Lobster Bisque.

If this one dish of Sookie's is so special that it bookends the entire series, surely it's worth a try, isn't it?

¾–1 lb	Frozen lobster tail
8 c	Water
2 T	Salt
2 T	Olive oil
1	Onion, medium, peeled, diced
3	Garlic cloves, peeled, minced
2	Carrots, peeled, finely chopped
3	Celery stalks, ends removed, finely chopped
2 T	Tomato paste
1 c	Sherry
2 t	Minced fresh thyme
⅓ c	Rice
½ c	Heavy cream
½ t	Salt
⅛ t	Cayenne pepper

Thaw lobster tail: Remove lobster tail from freezer. Let thaw at room temperature for 1 hour.

Boil lobster tail: Pour 8 cups water into large saucepan. Over high heat, bring to a boil. Add salt. Place lobster tail in water. Boil for about 10 minutes. When shell is bright red and meat is white rather than gray, remove tail from water, using tongs. Leave water in pot but remove from heat. Let lobster cool for 10 minutes.

Cut lobster tail: When lobster is cool enough to touch, use kitchen shears to cut up the center of the underside of the tail. Pull back shell on either side. Use a fork to remove all of the meat. Place it in a bowl and set aside. Return shell to water in pot. Over high heat, bring to a boil. Continue to boil until water has reduced to 4 cups. This is your lobster stock. Remove from heat and set aside. Discard shell.

Sauté vegetables: In another large saucepan or Dutch oven, heat olive oil over medium-high heat. Add onion, garlic, carrots, and celery. Sauté for 5 minutes, until onions are translucent. Add tomato paste and stir. Add sherry and thyme and stir until fully mixed.

Make soup: Add lobster stock to vegetable mixture. Cover and simmer for 1 hour. Add rice. Cover and simmer over medium heat for 30 minutes.

Blend soup: Working in batches, blend the soup in a blender until all vegetables and rice are dissolved. Return liquid to pan.

Make bisque: Add heavy cream, salt, and cayenne. Over medium heat, bring bisque to a simmer. Serve.

Makes 2–4 servings.

s1 e4

Tester— Liz Groff

CARAMELIZED SALMON

EMILY'S STAFF

Emily loves her maids when they start, then quickly finds one thing about them she hates—walking too loudly, walking too quietly, answering the door too slowly, speaking in Spanish with Rory. She soon fires them and moves on to the next. This maid's fatal mistake is putting sugar in everything, including salmon.

Although, should she really be faulted for adding a complex, sweet, nutty flavor to salmon? Try it and see whether or not you agree with Emily.

1 T	Sugar
1 T	Brown sugar
1 t	Kosher salt
½ t	Black pepper
1 lb	Salmon, with skin, cut into 3–4 fillets
2 T	Olive oil

Season fish: In a small bowl, combine sugars, salt, and pepper. By hand, rub the skinless sides of the salmon with sugar mixture.

Sauté fish: Add olive oil to deep skillet or large frying pan over medium-high heat. When oil becomes more liquid and moves easily around pan, it's ready. Add salmon, skin-side up. Sauté for 3 minutes. After salmon has sautéed for 1 minute, reduce heat to medium-low. After the full 3 minutes, turn fish over. Sauté for an additional 2 minutes.

Serve: Remove from pan onto a plate. Tent with aluminum foil. Let stand for 5 minutes. Serve.

Makes 4–6 servings.

s6e6

Tester—Meghan Fatticci

SEA BASS IN A LEMON DILL SAUCE

After his heart attack, Richard comes home from the hospital to a barrage of fish dishes. At some point Emily read an article about how good for the heart it is to eat fish, which led to her purchasing tons of fish from the Fish Man.

She also hired a celebrated chef to cook for them. Still, no matter how much the chef dresses up the fish dishes, Richard cannot stand them. After all, he loves steaks, lamb, and pasta dishes. No amount of Emily and Lorelai complimenting the lemon dill sauce is going to change his mind.

Is Richard right or is he just being a difficult patient? Would a fresh lemon dill sauce change your mind?

For sauce:

1½ c	Greek yogurt, plain
2 T	Olive oil
⅓ c	Lemon juice, freshly squeezed
2 t	Chopped fresh dill
½ t	Sea salt

For fish:

	Olive oil
1–2 lbs	Sea bass (8 oz per person)
	Salt and pepper
1	Lemon, thinly sliced, seeds removed

Make sauce: Combine all ingredients for sauce and mix well until fully combined. Refrigerate 30 minutes.

Prepare pan and oven: Coat bottom of baking dish with a thin layer of olive oil. Set aside. Ensure oven rack is positioned in center of oven. Preheat oven to 450°F.

Prepare fish: Coat fish generously with salt and pepper on both sides. Place fish in baking dish and top with slices of lemon.

Bake fish: Place baking dish in center of rack. Bake for 20 minutes. When fish is done it will be flaky but still moist. Remove from oven. Let rest for 10 minutes. Serve with sauce.

Makes 2–4 8-ounce servings.

Tester—Rebecca Broomall

Eat Like a Gilmore DAILY CRAVINGS

LOBSTER POTPIE

Sookie's infamous potpie makes its only appearance at the tasting she and Lorelai host for Emily. The actual party never happened, and the lobster potpie was never mentioned again.

It sounds too amazingly decadent to let it simply fade away, so here it is. Enjoy!

For crust:

4 c	Flour
2 t	Salt
⅔ c	Shortening, cold
1 c	Butter, cold
1 c	Ice water

For filling:

½ c	Cubed pancetta
2 T	Butter
½ c	Peeled and minced shallots
¼ c	Flour
1 T	Sherry
2 c	Fish or lobster stock
¼ t	Salt
⅛ t	Cayenne
⅛ t	Cinnamon
½ c	Heavy cream
1 c	Cooked and chopped lobster meat
2 lg	Carrots, peeled, chopped
1 lg	Zucchini, chopped
1	Potato, peeled, cubed (Yukon Gold recommended)

Prepare pie plate and oven: Set out 4 mini pie plates or 8 oz ramekins. Ensure the oven rack is in the middle position. Preheat oven to 400°F.

Make piecrust dough: In a medium mixing bowl, combine flour and salt. Add shortening and butter. Use a pastry cutter or dough cutter to cut the fats into the flour until the flour looks like little white peas. Add ¼ cup of water and continue to cut/mix dough using cutter. A dough will begin to form. If the dough seems dry or if substantial flour remains at the bottom of the bowl, add 1 or 2 additional tablespoons of water as needed. Continue adding water one tablespoon at a time until dough is soft but not mushy. Divide dough into ⅔ and ⅓. Take the ⅔ portion and divide into four even balls. These will be your bottom crusts. Take the ⅓ portion and divide into four even balls, as well. These will be your top crusts. Press each ball into a flat disc. Wrap each in plastic wrap and refrigerate for 30 minutes.

Roll out bottom crusts: Generously flour a flat work surface. Remove the dough for the four bottom crusts from refrigerator. Use a rolling pin to roll each ball of dough into an 8-inch circle. Place rolling pin onto the dough, toward one side edge. Fold the dough onto the rolling pin, then slowly roll the rolling pin so the dough loosely wraps around it. (If the dough is stuck to the work surface, use a dough cutter to gently scrape the dough off the surface as you go.) Position the rolling pin over the pie plate, then unroll the dough into the pie plate. Press the dough into position, making sure there are no air bubbles under the dough. Repeat with the other three balls of dough. Set aside.

Make gravy: In a large saucepan, deep skillet, or Dutch oven, fry pancetta over medium-high heat until crispy. Use a slotted spoon to remove meat from pan, while leaving oils in the pan. Add butter, melt it, and stir to combine with the pancetta oils. Add shallots and cook for 2–3 minutes. Once shallots turn medium brown, sprinkle with flour and stir. Once all flour has been absorbed, add sherry to pan.

Then add stock and spices. Stir until fully combined. Once stock begins to thicken, remove from heat and add heavy cream. Stir until fully combined. Add lobster and pancetta pieces. Set aside.

Roll top crusts: Generously flour a flat work surface. Remove the dough for the four top crusts from refrigerator. Use a rolling pin to roll each ball of dough into a 4-inch circle. Let sit until pies are filled.

Make potpies: Mix all of the prepared vegetables—carrots, zucchini, and potato—together. Then place roughly ¼ cup of raw vegetables into each prepared crust. Add ½ cup of the lobster mixture into each. Top each one with another ¼ cup of vegetables. Using the same method to move the crust dough, place a top crust onto each pie, lining up the edges with the bottom crusts. Crimp edges together with fork, crimping tool, or fingers. Cut several small slits in the top of each pie.

Bake potpies: Place on a cookie sheet (to catch overspills). Place cookie sheet in oven and bake for 45 minutes. Remove pies from oven once edges and tops are golden brown. Let stand at room temperature for 10 minutes. Serve.

Tester—Sarah Panizza

Eat Like a Gilmore DAILY CRAVINGS

SPAGHETTI & WHEAT BALLS

CONTRIBUTED BY GEROME HUERTA

Mrs. Kim makes this dish as a substitute after her gluten patties catch fire. She tells Lane, but Lane's not listening. She's too busy obsessing over the jug her mother wants her to send Dave in California. She thinks it symbolizes that she and Dave are supposed to marry. Lane holds off on sending the jug, but she worries over it for days before finally confronting her mother. Thankfully, Mrs. Kim is able to reassure her it was just a jug the whole time. No strings attached. But after the long discussion about it, the wheatballs are burned, too.

For sauce:

4	Garlic cloves, peeled, crushed
¼ c	Minced onion
2 T	Olive oil
¼ c	Finely chopped frozen spinach (thawed, with water removed)
2	29-oz cans tomato sauce
2	8-oz cans diced tomatoes with oil, garlic, and basil
4 T	Dried parsley
2 T	Dried oregano
1 T	Black pepper, or to taste
2 T	Sugar, or to taste
1 T	Salt, or to taste
4	Leaves basil, fresh, garnish

For wheatballs:

1½ c	Wheat flour
1 c	Italian bread crumbs
1 T	Dried oregano
1 T	Dried parsley
1 t	Granulated garlic
1 t	Dried basil
1 t	Crushed red pepper
¼ t	Celery salt

2	Cremini/brown mushrooms, finely chopped
¼ c	Peeled and diced onion
3	Garlic cloves, peeled, minced
3	Eggs
½ c	Vegetable broth, more as needed
2 T	Olive oil, *divided*

Make sauce:

Sauté onion and garlic: In a stockpot or Dutch oven, over medium heat, sauté garlic and onions in olive oil until soft and translucent.

Make sauce: Add in spinach, tomato sauce, diced tomatoes, parsley, oregano, and black pepper. Simmer for 20 minutes over medium heat, stirring often. Mix in sugar and salt to taste. Simmer for 2–3 minutes more, then remove from heat.

Make wheatballs:

Prepare pan and oven: Line a baking sheet with parchment paper or a silicone baking mat. Set aside. Ensure oven rack is in center position. Preheat oven to 375°F.

Make flour/herb mix: Blend wheat flour, bread crumbs, oregano, parsley, garlic, basil, crushed red pepper, and celery salt together in a food processor until it is fully combined. Place mixture in large bowl. Add mushrooms and onion. Use a wooden spoon to combine.

Sauté garlic: In a small saucepan, heat 1 tablespoon olive oil for 1–2 minutes. Add garlic. Sauté garlic cloves just until they change to golden brown. Remove from heat and set aside.

Mix wet ingredients: Whisk eggs. Add vegetable broth and whisk until combined.

Make wheatballs: Add remaining 1 tablespoon olive oil to dry ingredients, then slowly add broth mixture, stirring with a wooden spoon to combine. Continue to mix until well-blended. With the resulting mixture, form 1½–2-inch balls, rolling them by hand. Place each ball on the prepared pan with ½ inch space between each ball. Repeat until all dough has been used.

Bake wheatballs: Cover pan with aluminum foil. Place pan in oven. Bake for 15 minutes. Pull pan from oven and remove aluminum foil. Place pan back in oven. Bake for an additional 15 minutes. Test for doneness by breaking open 1 wheatball— it should be cooked through, not doughy. If the center is still doughy, cook for an additional 5 minutes. Remove from oven. Using tongs or a large spoon, carefully add wheatballs to sauce and simmer.

Serving suggestions: Serve wheatballs and sauce over cooked pasta*: capellini, thin spaghetti, or angel-hair pasta recommended. Tear basil leaves into small bits and place on top of completed dish. Shaved Parmesan adds a nice touch, also.

This dish works very well with zucchini or squash pasta, too!

Makes 4–6 servings.

LASAGNA

When Liz moves back to Stars Hollow, we start to learn more personal things about Luke. For instance, that he's an accomplished cook, that he cooks in his spare time, and that he's nicknamed "the lasagna king" because he once completely obsessed over lasagna, trying to find the perfect recipe.

This recipe seems like one Luke would create. It offers a fresh, healthy twist on a traditional Italian foundation. Mangia! Mangia!

10 lb	Roma tomatoes
3 t	Salt, *divided*
3 c	Ricotta cheese
1 t	Kosher salt
1½ t	Pepper, *divided*
¾ c	Minced fresh parsley, *divided*
½ lb	Italian sausage, sweet, hot, or a combination of both
½ lb	Ground beef
2 T	Olive oil
2 c	Peeled and diced white onion
12	Garlic cloves, peeled, minced
1 c	Red wine
1 box	Lasagna noodles
2 c	Parmesan cheese
1 c/16 oz	Mozzarella, fresh & packed in water, sliced into 8–10 thin ovals

Prep pans: Prepare two stockpots or Dutch ovens by filling each with water until ⅔ full. Pot #1: Place on a burner over high heat. Pot #2: Place on another burner but do not turn on heat. While Pot #1 is heating up, move on to the next step.

Prep tomatoes: Cut off the stem end (top) and cut an X into the other end (bottom) of each tomato.

Blanch tomatoes: Once the water in the first pot comes to a boil, add 1 teaspoon salt to Pot #1 and place a few ice cubes into the Pot #2 to make it as cold as possible. Carefully drop 6–8 tomatoes into the boiling water for 3 minutes. Using a slotted spoon or tongs, scoop out each tomato, placing it into the cold water in Pot #2. After 3 minutes, scoop tomatoes out of cold water and place them into a bowl. Repeat for all tomatoes. Cool tomatoes while you carry out the following two steps.

Prep ricotta: In a medium mixing bowl, add ricotta, 1 teaspoon kosher salt, ½ teaspoon pepper, and 3 tablespoons parsley. Mix thoroughly. Cover and refrigerate 1 hour.

Cook meats: In a Dutch oven, add sausage and ground beef. If sausage is in casing, remove casing before placing meat in pan. During the cooking process, use a wooden spoon to crumble meat into smallest pieces possible. Once meat is fully browned, use a slotted spoon to remove it from pan. Place it into a medium bowl, cover it with foil, and set aside. Turn off heat, but leave the grease from the meats in the pot.

Peel tomatoes: Take each blanched tomato and peel off its outer skin. Discard the skins. Place peeled tomatoes into a large bowl. Test them to see how hot they are on the inside. If they are not too hot to the touch, then squeeze each tomato with your hands, into the bowl. Set aside.

Make sauce: Over medium-high heat, reheat the pot

containing the grease from the meats. Add olive oil and mix thoroughly. Add onion and garlic. Cook until onion is translucent. Add tomatoes and red wine. Stir until mixed. Bring to a boil and continue to boil for 10 minutes. Then reduce heat to simmer sauce, uncovered, for 30 minutes, stirring occasionally.

Blend sauce: To break down the large chunks of tomato in the sauce, working in batches, use a slotted spoon to remove large pieces of tomato. Place tomato pieces in blender and blend until smooth. Repeat until sauce is free of all large chunks. Add parsley. Place cover on pot and continue to simmer for at least 1 more hour. During this time, you may move on to the next step.

Boil noodles: Fill a stockpot or Dutch oven with water until pot is two-thirds full. Bring to a boil. Add 2 teaspoons of salt to water. Then carefully place each lasagna noodle into the water. Crisscross the noodles in the pot so they won't stick together. Boil the noodles for 8 minutes. Noodles will still be very al dente. Remove from heat. Get a large bowl and a pair of tongs or a fork. Carefully remove each noodle from the water and place it into the large bowl. Once all noodles are in the bowl, discard water in pot.

Prepare pan and oven: Ideally, use a 10x14 glass baking dish for this recipe. You may also use an 8x10 inch glass baking dish, though not all ingredients will fit. Set pan aside. Ensure oven rack is positioned in the middle oven. Preheat oven to 350°F.

Continued on the next page . . .

Tester—Gabi Faber

Eat Like a Gilmore DAILY CRAVINGS

Assemble lasagna:

Choose one method.

For rolled lasagna:

Pour 2 cups of the sauce into the bottom of the baking dish, ensuring the dish is covered evenly. On a flat work surface, lay out a paper towel. Place 3 lasagna noodles onto the paper towel. Using a second paper towel, rub the center of each noodle to partially dry it. This will help the ricotta adhere to the noodle. Cover the center of each noodle with a light later of ricotta. Then spoon, evenly, a couple tablespoons of the meat onto the noodles. Sprinkle Parmesan cheese onto the meat. Then, starting at one end, gently roll each noodle until it looks like a spool. Place the noodle into the pan, seam-side down. Open side of the noodle should face the side of the pan. Repeat for all noodles. Cover noodles with sauce. Sprinkle parmesan onto top of entire lasagna. Place mozzarella slices on top.

For layered lasagna:

Pour 2 cups of the sauce into the bottom of the baking dish, ensuring the dish is covered evenly. Place noodles flat on the bottom of the pan, in a row, until entire bottom is covered. Add a light layer of ricotta, then top with a layer of meat. Sprinkle Parmesan cheese onto the meat layer. Add another layer of sauce. Repeat the layering of noodles, ricotta, meat, and Parmesan. Add one more layer of noodles. Cover with sauce. Sprinkle with Parmesan. Cover with slices of mozzarella.

Bake lasagna: Place baking dish in oven, uncovered. Bake at 350°F for 1 hour. Lasagna will be very bubbly with crisp edges when done. Remove from oven. Let cool for 15 minutes. Serve.

Makes 6–8 servings.

MOROCCAN MEATBALL TAGINE

AL'S PANCAKE WORLD

The fun of International Grab Bag Night at Al's Pancake World is the surprise of it. Which country is my dinner from? Rory always thinks her dinner is Moroccan. Is this because she cannot tell the difference between various countries' cuisine? Or is it because Al uses the same twelve ingredients in everything he makes? We may never know the answer. BUT, we can now celebrate our own Moroccan night at home. Besseha!

For meatballs (kefka):

3 T	Olive oil, *divided*
1	Medium onion, peeled and minced
2 t	Peeled and minced garlic
¾ lb	Extra-lean ground beef (96/4)
¾ lb	Lean ground lamb
¼ c	Finely chopped cilantro
¼ c	Finely chopped fresh mint
1 T	Kosher salt
2 t	Paprika, sweet
2 t	Ground cumin
1 t	Ground ginger
½ t	Black pepper
½ t	Cayenne pepper, *optional*
½ t	Cinnamon
1	Egg

For tagine:

2 T	Olive oil, if needed
2	Onions, peeled, halved, then sliced
2	Carrots, peeled, halved, length-wise, then cut into 1-inch diagonal pieces
1 T	Peeled and minced garlic
3 T	Tomato paste
2 c	Beef stock
1	Yellow bell pepper, stemmed, seeds removed, julienned
1	Red bell pepper, stemmed, seeds removed, julienned
12	Dried apricots
12	Prunes, pitted
½ c	Kalamata olives, pitted
½–2 t	Crushed red pepper (adjust based on personal taste)
2 t	Kosher salt
1 t	Paprika, sweet
1 t	Ground cumin
1 t	Black pepper
1 t	Ground coriander
½ t	Ground cinnamon
½ t	Ground cloves
½ t	Ground cardamom
½ t	Ground ginger
½ t	Ground turmeric
¼ c	Lemon juice, freshly squeezed
1 T	Lemon zest
½ c	Coarsely chopped mint leaves

For serving:

Couscous, cooked

Mint, cilantro, or parsley, chopped, garnish

Almonds, sliced or slivered

Greek-style yogurt

Sauté onions and garlic: In a Dutch oven, heat 1 tablespoon olive oil over medium-high heat for 2 minutes. Add onions. Sauté onions for 1 minute, until they begin to give off water. Add garlic. Sauté for 1 minute more. Remove from heat. Let cool.

Make meatballs: In a large bowl, combine beef, lamb, herbs, and spices. Add egg. Mix with hands until ingredients are thoroughly, evenly combined. Add cooled onions and garlic. Continue to mix until onions and garlic are evenly incorporated. Form mixture into 1½–2-inch meatballs, approximately the size of golf balls.

Sear meatballs: Add 2 tablespoons olive oil to a Dutch oven or large frying pan over medium heat. Heat for 2–3 minutes. Add meatballs, gently, in a single layer. As meatballs cook, use a wooden spoon or silicone spatula to turn them, carefully, so they cook evenly on all sides. Once meatballs are browned on all sides, use a slotted spoon to remove them from pan. Set aside.

Prepare oven: Ensure oven rack is in the second to lowest position. Preheat oven to 180°F.

Cook vegetables: The pan should have roughly ¼ cup of liquid at the bottom. If your pan doesn't have much liquid, add 2 tablespoons more olive oil to pan. Add onions and carrots. Cook until onions become translucent. Add garlic and cook for 1 minute. In a small bowl or large measuring cup, mix tomato paste into stock. Add spices to broth and mix. Add broth to pan. Add meatballs back to pan. Fold in dried fruits, olives, and mint leaves. Add lemon juice and zest. Gently stir to combine. Let cook for 5 minutes.

Bake: Place lid on Dutch oven, or transfer to a covered baking dish or tagine. Place in oven. Bake for 20 minutes. Remove from oven. Let stand for 5 minutes. Spoon over cooked couscous. Garnish with chopped cilantro, mint, or parsley. Add almonds and yogurt. Serve.

Makes 25–30 meatballs for 4–6 servings.

TUNA LOAF
CONTRIBUTED BY GEROME HUERTA

Liz and TJ invite Luke over for a home-cooked meal, completely forgetting their oven is broken. After white Russian cocktail hour and the fancy Jell-O first course are over, Luke ends up driving to the store and making dinner for everyone.

3	Eggs
5 t	Mayonnaise
2 T	Vegetable oil
1 T	Lemon juice, freshly squeezed, *optional*
⅓ c	Peeled and diced yellow or white onion
½ t	Salt
1 T	Black pepper
2 T	Parsley
2 T	Shredded Romano, Parmesan, or cheddar, cheese
2	24-oz cans tuna, packed in water, drained but not dry
1 c	Italian bread crumbs*

*To make your own Italian bread crumbs. Mix all ingredients:

1 c	Plain bread crumbs
½ t	Salt
½ t	Black pepper
½ t	Parsley flakes
½ t	Granulated garlic
½ t	Dried thyme
¼ t	Dried basil
¼ t	Dried oregano
¼ t	Dried sage
¼ t	Dried coriander

Prepare pan and oven: Coat the inside of a medium loaf pan with nonstick spray. Set aside. Ensure oven rack is positioned in center of oven. Preheat oven to 375°F.

Mix ingredients: In a large mixing bowl, beat eggs. Add mayonnaise, oil, lemon juice, onion, salt, pepper, parsley, and cheese into eggs (everything except tuna and bread crumbs). Mix using a wooden spoon or a silicone spatula. Once all ingredients are mixed well together, add tuna and mix. Then add bread crumbs and mix. At this point it's best to use hands to finish mixing.

Bake loaf: Scoop mixture into loaf pan, distributing it evenly. Cover the pan loosely with aluminum foil. Place pan in oven. Bake for 40 minutes. Remove from oven. Let stand for 10 minutes. Cut into 1-inch slices. Serve.

Serving suggestions: Tastes great with ketchup, cocktail sauce, or a mixture of ¼ cup ketchup, ⅛ cup yellow mustard, and 2–3 tablespoons sriracha!

Variation: This recipe will also work for tuna patties. Instead of baking, form mixture into patties. Fry patties in pan until browned on both sides and add a slice of cheese, if you please.

Makes 4 servings.

Ice Creams
& Old-Fashioned Sodas

APPLE CIDER
ICE CREAM

SOOKIE'S KITCHEN

Weeks after Lorelai has called off her engagement to Max, a wedding gift arrives in fancy, bouffant white wrapping. Turns out, it's an ice cream maker—a Musso Lussino 4080 from Italy, which retails for over $1,000. The moment Sookie recognizes what it is, she's immediately inspired to turn Jackson's apple crop into apple cider ice cream. But the question remains, who sent the ice cream maker?

For apple cider swirl:

6	Apples, peeled, cored, sliced, Granny Smith recommended
1 c	Sugar
2 T	Lemon juice, freshly squeezed
1 T	Ground cinnamon
½ t	Kosher or Sea salt
¼ t	Ground cloves
1 T	Cornstarch

For ice cream:

1½ c	Milk
1¼ c	Heavy cream
1 c	Sugar
3	Egg yolks
1 t	Vanilla extract

Masticate apples: Place peeled apple slices in a large bowl. Sprinkle with sugar. Add lemon juice, cinnamon, salt, and cloves. Gently fold the slices 2–3 times to combine. Let stand at room temperature for 1 hour.

Make custard: Add milk, cream, sugar, yolks, and vanilla extract to medium saucepan. Heat over medium-high heat. Use a wooden spoon, silicone spatula, or silicone-covered whisk to stir often. As mixture begins to boil, stir continuously and remove from heat. Pour mixture into a heat- and cold-proof bowl. Place a piece of plastic wrap directly onto the top of the mixture. Place bowl into refrigerator for 4 hours or into freezer for 30 minutes.

Make apple cider syrup: Use a slotted spoon to remove apple slices from bowl. Pour apple juices into measuring cup. You should have ¾ cup to 1 cup of juice. (If you have less, wait a little longer for the apple slices to produce more juice.) Add cornstarch to juice and stir to combine. Pour juice into small saucepan. Stir the juice constantly over medium-high heat. Bring the juice to a boil. Reduce heat and continue stirring. Once juice starts to thicken and looks like a smooth, dark brown syrup, remove from heat. Pour into a small container, cover, and refrigerate.

Churn ice cream: Once custard has cooled completely, pour it into ice cream canister. Turn on machine and churn for 30 minutes. Custard will take on the consistency of soft-serve ice cream. Turn off machine.

Freeze ice cream: Immediately after churning, scoop ⅓ of the ice cream out of the canister, into a loaf pan. Spoon half the apple cider syrup onto the ice cream, and gently spread into a layer. Repeat with the second third of ice cream and remaining syrup. Top with the final third of ice cream. Place a piece of plastic wrap directly onto the top of the ice cream. Cover pan with aluminum foil. Freeze 6 hours or overnight. Serve.

Makes 3–4 servings, or enough for 1 wallowing session.

Tester—Andrea Blatt

CHOCOLATE CHIP COOKIE DOUGH
ICE CREAM

AT HOME

One of the most important life lessons *Gilmore Girls* teaches us, apart from consuming massive amounts of snack food while watching TV, is to wallow. It teaches us that when something bad happens, we need to take some time to feel all of our sad feelings. We need to wallow, while eating massive amounts of snack foods—primarily ice cream.

There's no better wallowing ice cream than chocolate chip cookie dough—it's ice cream and chocolate and raw cookie dough all in one!

For the cookie dough:

⅓ c	Butter, softened
¼ c	Sugar
¼ c	Brown sugar
½ t	Vanilla
½ c	Flour
2 T	Milk
½ c	Mini chocolate chips

For the ice cream:

3	Egg yolks
1 c	Sugar
1½ c	Whole milk
1¼ c	Heavy cream
1 T	Vanilla
½ c	Mini chocolate chips

Make cookie dough: In medium mixing bowl, add butter and sugars. Cream together using a hand mixer. Add vanilla and mix. Add flour and mix. Add milk gradually until dough reaches desired consistency. Fold in chocolate chips until evenly distributed throughout. Dough may be served as is, immediately, or used as a mix-in for ice cream. To use as a mix-in, wrap in plastic wrap and refrigerate for at least 30 minutes.

Make custard: Add yolks, sugar, milk, cream, and vanilla to large saucepan or Dutch oven. Heat over medium-high heat. Use a wooden spoon or silicone spatula to stir often. As mixture begins to boil, stir continuously and remove from heat. Pour mixture into a heat- and cold-proof bowl. Place a piece of plastic wrap directly onto the top of the mixture. Place bowl into refrigerator for 4 hours or into freezer for 30 minutes.

Churn ice cream: Once custard has cooled completely, pour it into ice cream canister. Turn on machine and churn. After 20 minutes, the custard should be close to the con-sistency of soft-serve ice cream—with no liquid. If it hasn't reached that consistency, continue to churn until it does. As ice cream reaches the desired consistency, add in chocolate chips and churn. Then add in cookie dough in ½ teaspoon size pieces. When all dough has been mixed into ice cream, turn off machine.

Freeze ice cream: Immediately after churning, scoop the ice cream out of the canister into a loaf pan. Place a piece of plastic wrap directly onto the top of the ice cream. Cover pan with aluminum foil. Freeze 6 hours or overnight. Serve.

Makes 3–4 servings, or enough for 1 wallowing session.

s1 e17

Tester—Rebecca Blanchette

ROCKY ROAD
ICE CREAM

Through Logan, we find out wallowing is not reserved exclusively for the ladies. When he is clamoring to get Rory back and she agrees to have dinner with him, he makes an uncharacteristically desperate plea to her to please not cancel. He goes on to describe to her what would happen if she did cancel —a scenario involving him eating a huge amount of rocky road ice cream while watching a Nora Ephron movie. That's right, Logan, super-coiffed-billionaire-heir-Logan, would be camped out in bed with ice cream and a sappy movie. Clearly, wallowing works for the guys, too!

¾ c	Chocolate bar pieces or chips, 55–70% cacao
3	Egg yolks
1 c	Sugar
1½ c	Whole milk
1¼ c	Heavy cream
¾ c	Chopped or sliced nuts
¾ c	Chocolate chips, semi-sweet, mini
¾ c	Marshmallows, mini

Make custard: Place chocolate pieces or chips into a large, heat-proof bowl. In a large saucepan or Dutch oven add yolks, sugar, milk, and cream. Heat over medium-high heat. Use a wooden spoon or silicone spatula to stir often. As mixture begins to boil, stir continuously and remove from heat. Pour over the chocolate. Let stand for 5 minutes to melt chocolate. Stir to blend. Continue to stir until all pieces of chocolate are melted and mixture is fully combined. Cover with a piece of plastic wrap. Refrigerate for 4 hours or freeze for 30 minutes.

Churn ice cream: Pour chilled custard into canister of ice cream maker/machine. Churn for 30 minutes. Custard should take on the consistency of soft serve ice cream. After 30 minutes, if custard is still watery or contains liquid, continue to churn until it reaches the proper consistency. Before turning off machine, add in nuts, chocolate chips, and marshmallows, allowing for each to churn into ice cream before adding the next. Once all add-ins have been churned into the ice cream, turn off the machine.

Freeze ice cream: Immediately after churning, scoop the ice cream out of the canister, into a loaf pan. Place a piece of plastic wrap directly onto the top of the ice cream. Cover pan with aluminum foil. Freeze 6 hours or overnight. Serve.

Makes 3–4 servings, or enough for 1 wallowing session.

s6e13 *Tester*—Alyssa Race

Eat Like a Gilmore DAILY CRAVINGS

PEPPERMINT STICK
ICE CREAM

Taylor just opened his new soda shop and already he's in a heated argument with Luke because he failed to ask Luke if he could install a huge picture window between his store and the diner. Meanwhile, on the menu board, one flavor of ice cream instantly jumps out—peppermint stick, typically a December-only flavor, is available in September at Taylor's. Stars Hollow really is a magical place!

For the ice cream:

8	Egg yolks
2 c	Sugar
3 c	Whole milk
2 c	Heavy cream
1 T	Peppermint extract
½ t	Salt
20	Peppermint candies, round, unwrapped

For the optional peppermint candy add-in:

1 c	Water
40	Peppermint candies, round, unwrapped
2 T	Butter
2 T	Heavy cream

Make custard: Add yolks, sugar, milk, cream, extract, and salt to large saucepan or Dutch oven. Heat over medium-high heat. Use a wooden spoon or silicone spatula to stir often. As mixture begins to boil, stir continuously and remove from heat. Pour mixture into a heat- and cold-proof bowl. Place a piece of plastic wrap directly onto the top of the mixture. Place bowl into refrigerator for 4 hours or into freezer for 30 minutes.

Prep add-in: In a medium saucepan, add water and candies. Bring the water to a boil over medium-high heat, stirring occasionally. Once the candies have fully melted, continue to boil to reduce the water content until it is approximately half. (Watch for the point when the white portion of the candies disappears entirely.) Add butter. Stir until fully melted and combined. Add cream. Stir to combine. Remove from heat. Pour into a heat- and cold-proof bowl. Refrigerate for 1 hour or freeze for 15 minutes, until candy is cooled all the way through.

Prep peppermint candies: Place candies in a plastic bag. Seal the bag. Using a rolling pin, a mallet, or a hammer crush the candies until they are broken into a combination of tiny pieces and dust. Pour candy into a small bowl. Set aside.

Churn ice cream: Once custard has cooled completely, pour it into ice cream canister. Turn on machine and churn. After 10 minutes of churning, add the add-in candy. Use a fork or a teaspoon to add gumdrop-sized balls of the add-in into the ice cream. While the ice cream continues to churn, drop them in, one at a time. After ice cream has been churning for 15 minutes, add the crushed peppermint candy. After 20 minutes, the custard should be close to the consistency of soft-serve ice cream—with no liquid. If it hasn't reached that consistency, continue to churn until it does.

Freeze ice cream: Immediately after churning, scoop the ice cream out of the canister, into a loaf pan. Place a piece of plastic wrap directly onto the top of the ice cream. Cover pan with aluminum foil. Freeze 6 hours or overnight. Serve.

Makes 3–4 servings, or enough for 1 wallowing session.

Tester—Alyssa Race

STRAWBERRY ICE CREAM

As tradition dictates, the new additions to the *Yale Daily News* wear hats made out of newspaper. Rory makes a perfectly passable triangle hat, Glenn rubberbands a piece of newspaper to his head, and Paris wins the day by donning a lovely newspaper bonnet after getting a little help from Martha Stewart. Their editor, Doyle, who just got turned down for a job at Time Magazine, takes out his anger by having a mini fit that his strawberry ice cream has chunks of strawberries in it.

When you saw this scene, were you dumbfounded like Rory, or did you completely get Doyle's point? Strawberry chunks or no strawberry chunks?

5 c	Strawberries, washed
2 c	Sugar, *divided*
1 T	Lemon juice, freshly squeezed, *optional*
4 T	Cornstarch
1½ c	Whole milk, cold
1¼ c	Heavy cream
1 t	Vanilla extract

Masticate strawberries: Remove stems from strawberries. Slice each one into 2–4 generous slices, depending on how large the berry is. Place strawberry slices in large mixing bowl. Cover with 1 cup of sugar and lemon juice. Use a fork to gently mix the sugar into the strawberries. Cover and place in refrigerator for 6 hours or overnight.

Strain juices: Strain the strawberries and reserve 1 cup of the juices. Cut 1 cup of strawberry solids into small pieces. Set aside.

Make custard: Stir cornstarch into cold milk until fully dissolved. In a medium saucepan, add remaining sugar, cream, and milk/cornstarch mixture. Cook custard over medium-high heat. Use a wooden spoon or silicone spatula to stir often. Once mixture begins to boil, it will also start to thicken. Remove from heat. Continue to stir. Add 1 cup strawberry juices and vanilla extract. Combine until mixture is fully blended. Cover and refrigerate for 6 hours or freeze for 1 hour.

Churn ice cream: Pour chilled custard into canister of ice cream maker/machine. Churn for 30 minutes. Custard should take on the consistency of soft serve ice cream. After 30 minutes, if custard is still watery or contains liquid, continue to churn until it reaches the proper consistency. Before turning off machine, add in strawberry pieces (this step is optional). Once strawberries have been fully incorporated into ice cream, turn off machine.

Freeze ice cream: Immediately after churning, scoop the ice cream out of the canister, into a loaf pan. Place a piece of plastic wrap directly onto the top of the ice cream. Cover pan with aluminum foil. Freeze 6 hours or overnight. Serve.

Makes 3–4 servings, or enough for 1 wallowing session.

PASSION FRUIT
SORBET

EMILY'S STAFF

It was a Friday night dinner we would not soon forget. The Gilmores were frustrated with each other, and no one held anything back. Rory had allowed Christopher to pay for Yale, and her grandparents were offended, to say the least. Richard and Emily had double-crossed Lorelai when they changed the plan to convince Rory to go back to school. Lorelai, well, Emily was always irritated with Lorelai. Tensions were high, but suddenly, the family agreed on one thing: dessert. The delicious passion fruit sorbet, homemade by Emily's maid-of-the-moment, Theresa, cooled the heated atmosphere and calmed the arguing Gilmores.

You'll love this delightful palette cleanser before your after-dinner coffee, or your after-lunch coffee, or your midnight coffee. Any time is a good time for sorbet.

1 c	Sugar
2 c	Water
¾ c	Passion fruit, strained fresh pulp (from 10–11 passion fruits) or passion fruit puree
	Strawberries, garnish, *optional*

Make simple syrup: In medium saucepan, combine sugar and water. Over medium-high heat, stir with wooden spoon or silicone spatula until sugar is fully dissolved. Remove from heat. Stir in passion fruit pulp or passion fruit puree, until fully blended.

Chill: Transfer mixture to a cold-proof bowl. Cover with lid or plastic wrap. Refrigerate mixture a minimum of 4 hours. To accelerate process, mixture may be kept in freezer for up to 30 minutes. Once mixture is cold, it's ready to churn.

Churn: Pour mixture into prepped ice cream maker. Turn on and churn for 20 minutes. Once the liquid has changed form by turning into a dense slushy consistency, it's ready to freeze.

Freeze: Transfer slushy mixture out of ice cream canister, into a loaf pan. Use spatula or wooden spoon to distribute in pan evenly and smooth top. Place plastic wrap directly on top so no air can access the sorbet as it freezes. For best results, freeze overnight.

Serve: Scoop sorbet into individual bowls. Garnish with strawberries. Serve.

Makes 3–4 servings.

s6 e13
Intro by Jessica Wheeler
Tester—Jessica Wheeler

OLDE FASHIONED
SODA DRINKS

Do you love Taylor? Hate him? Love to hate him? For all of his "power" in town, why can't he approach business dealings in a straightforward manner? When he wanted to open an old-fashioned candy store next to Luke's, rather than bringing it up to Luke and discussing it like two respectable business owners, instead he launches an elaborate roundabout plan. He sends a couple boys and Kirk into Luke's asking for soda drinks, which he knows are not on Luke's menu—a chocolate phosphate, an egg cream, and a black cow. After the first ask, Luke's confused. After the second, he's suspicious. By the third, he knows who's behind the charade—Taylor.

Still, in the end, Taylor got his way, as he usually does.

Black Cow:

12 oz	Root beer
3 T	Chocolate syrup
3	Scoops vanilla ice cream
	Whipped cream
1	Maraschino cherry

To make: Pour 3 ounces of root beer into a tall glass. Add chocolate syrup and stir until syrup is fully incorporated. Add the remaining root beer. Scoop ice cream into the root beer. Top with whipped cream and a cherry. Serve.

Chocolate Phosphate:

4 T	Chocolate syrup
12 oz	Seltzer water
1 t	Acid phosphate
	Ice

To make: Pour chocolate syrup into tall glass. Add seltzer water, then add acid phosphate. Stir. Add ice. Serve.

Egg Cream:

4 T	Chocolate syrup
½ c	Milk
12 oz	Seltzer water
	Ice

To make: Add chocolate syrup to tall glass. Pour in milk. Stir to combine. Add seltzer water and gently stir. Add ice. Serve.

Tester—Rebecca Blanchette

Cookies
& Candies

BISCOTTI

The girls have successfully fought off the Sandinistas (not really) and have returned from Europe. Their first morning back they head out to distribute the gifts they picked up for all their friends. Armed with a little bag of biscotti they picked up in Milan, Italy, they walk to Luke's. Unbeknownst to them, the leisurely week they've planned filled with Sephora runs and *Godfather* movie marathons will be cut short, since Rory read the schedule wrong. She needs to be at Yale in two days! Hopefully, they brought home enough biscotti to get them through all the frantic errands.

For biscotti:

2 c	Flour
1 t	Baking powder
4 T	Butter, softened
½ c	Sugar
2	Eggs
1 T	Lemon zest
½ t	Anise extract
¼ c	Sliced or slivered almonds, toasted

For glaze:

½ c	Powdered sugar
1 t	Lemon juice
1½ t	Light corn syrup
1 t	Milk

Prepare pan and oven: Cover a baking sheet with parchment paper or a silicone baking mat. Set aside. Ensure oven rack is positioned in center of oven. Preheat oven to 350℉.

Combine dry ingredients: In medium bowl, combine flour and baking powder. Set aside.

Combine wet ingredients: In a larger mixing bowl, combine butter and sugar. Using an electric hand mixer, beat the two together until fully combined and creamy. Beat in eggs, one at a time. Add lemon zest and anise extract. Beat to combine.

Make dough: Gradually add the dry ingredients to the wet ingredients, beating after each addition. Once fully combined, fold in almonds using a wooden spoon or silicone spatula.

Bake biscotti: Turn out dough onto prepared pan. Form dough into one large, rectangular mound, roughly an inch tall. Bake in oven for 20 minutes.

Cool and cut biscotti: After 20 minutes, remove pan from oven. Reduce oven temperature to 275℉. Allow biscotti to cool for 20 minutes. Remove from pan, place on cutting board. Using a serrated knife, cut biscotti into ¾-inch strips.

Bake biscotti again: Place cut biscotti back onto pan, with each piece on its side. Place pan in oven. Bake for 40 minutes. Remove pan from oven. Let biscotti cool for 10 minutes before moving them to a cooling rack.

Make glaze: In a small bowl, combine powdered sugar, lemon juice, and corn syrup. Add milk as needed to get the desired consistency.

Glaze biscotti: Drizzle glaze onto biscotti. Let biscotti sit for 30 minutes to allow glaze to harden. Serve.

Makes 12–15 biscotti.

s4 e1

Tester—Lynn Tomei

CHOCOLATE BISCOTTI

Rory's father, Christopher, makes his first appearance riding into town on his Indian motorcycle and setting all of Stars Hollow into a gossip frenzy. Lorelai, having mixed feelings about his visit, needs to talk it out with someone other than Rory. She turns to Sookie. In the kitchen at the Independence Inn the two have a girlfriend-to-girlfriend talk. First things first, Sookie starts the talk by handing Lorelai a chocolate biscotto and teaching her to dunk it into her coffee before she eats it.

Take a lesson from Sookie. Dip one of these into hot coffee or milk, then take a bite.

2 c	Flour
½ c	Cocoa powder
1 t	Baking soda
1 t	Salt
8 T	Butter, softened
⅔ c	Sugar
2	Eggs
2 t	Vanilla extract
1 T	Amaretto
1 c	Mini chocolate chips
¾ c	Hazelnuts

Prepare pan and oven: Line a baking sheet with parchment paper or a silicone baking mat. Set aside. Ensure oven rack is positioned in center of oven. Preheat oven to 350°F.

Mix dry ingredients: In a medium bowl, combine flour, cocoa, baking soda, and salt. Use a fork to gently blend ingredients. Set aside.

Mix wet ingredients: In a large mixing bowl, combine butter and sugar. Use an electric hand mixer on medium speed to beat the two together until creamy. Add eggs, one at a time, beating after each one. Add vanilla and amaretto and beat to combine.

Make dough: Gradually add the dry ingredients to the wet ingredients, beating to combine after each addition. Use a wooden spoon or silicone spatula to fold in chocolate chips and nuts.

Bake dough: Turn dough out onto baking sheet. Divide the dough into two equal halves. Form each half into a 10-inch-long, 4-inch-wide mound. Place pan in oven. Bake for 20 minutes. Remove from oven. Let cool. Reduce oven setting to 270°F.

Cut biscotti and bake: Use a serrated knife to slice each mound into 1-inch strips. Place each strip on its side on the baking sheet. Place pan in oven. Bake for 40 minutes. Remove from oven. Let cool.

Serve.

Makes 18–20 biscotti.

Tester—Ashley Scarborough

RUM BALLS

Since Lorelai's been working 'round the clock, a very pregnant Sookie forces Lorelai to go out for a girls' night. They wind up at Weston's. When Rory joins them, she walks in to find Lorelai sitting at a table. Next to her is Sookie, asleep.

Lorelai and Rory move to a different table, letting Sookie sleep. Rory reveals her feelings for Logan and the fact that she's having sex with Logan. Lorelai, a little taken off guard, but happy to have her daughter confiding in her, wants to celebrate their talk by doing shots. This is the closest thing they could find in a bakery—rum balls.

1 box	Vanilla wafers, crushed
1½ c	Chopped roasted, unsalted pecans
1 c	Powdered sugar, *divided*
3 T	Cocoa powder
½ c	Spiced rum
3 T	Honey

Mix dough: In a medium mixing bowl, combine wafers, pecans, ¾ cup powdered sugar, cocoa, rum, and honey. Mix together using a wooden spoon.

Make rum balls: Roll dough into 1–1½-inch balls—approximately the size of a Ping-Pong ball. Add the remaining ¼ cup powdered sugar to a shallow bowl or plate. Roll each ball in sugar to coat. Serve.

Makes 30–40 rum balls.

Tester— Shannon Huffman

ANGEL WINGS
WITH DIPPING SAUCE

For Rory's sixteenth birthday party, Sookie makes these traditional European fried pastries. This is an interesting choice, because angel wings are typically reserved for Christmas and the week before Lent begins. By serving them in October, Sookie shows us these treats are versatile and great any time of year. So don't limit yourself—make these any time you feel they'll add a little light sweetness to an event.

For angel wings:

5	Egg yolks
2 T	Sugar
¼ t	Salt
3 T	Heavy cream, sour cream, or Greek-style yogurt
2 T	Whiskey
1 t	Vanilla
1 t	Lemon zest
1 t	Orange zest
1¼–1½ c	Flour
1 qt	Canola oil, for frying
1–2 c	Powdered sugar

For dipping sauce:

1 c	Fresh blueberries
3 T	Water
1 t	Lemon zest
3 T	Honey
1 T	Cornstarch
3 T	Lemon juice, freshly squeezed, cold

Make dough: In a medium mixing bowl using an electric hand mixer on medium-low speed, combine egg yolks, sugar, salt, cream, whiskey, vanilla, and zests. Gradually add flour. Once all flour has been added, if dough still feels sticky, add 2 tablespoons of flour at a time until dough is soft and not sticky. Knead dough for 5 minutes.

Roll and cut dough: Dust a flat work surface with flour. Roll out dough until it is very thin, about ⅛ of an inch. Cut dough into strips 1 inch by 4 inches. Cut a 1-inch slit down the center of each strip, lengthwise, then pull one end of the dough through the slit to make the "wings." Set aside.

Set up drying rack: Stack two paper towels on a plate, then place a cooling rack on the paper towels. This is where you'll place the cookies after they are fried.

Fry cookies: In a stockpot or Dutch oven, heat oil to 350–360°F. In batches, carefully lower cookies into oil. Use a wooden spoon or silicone spatula to turn cookies. Once cookies are light golden brown on all sides, use a slotted spoon to remove them from oil. Place them on the drying rack. Dust them with powdered sugar.

Make dipping sauce: In a small saucepan, combine blueberries, water, lemon zest, and honey. Over medium heat, stirring occasionally, bring to a boil. While blueberries are boiling, use a muddler or a potato masher to break down the berries. Reduce heat to low. Stir cornstarch into lemon juice until fully dissolved. Pour lemon juice into blueberries. Stir until sauce thickens. Remove from heat.

Serve: Serve cookies with sauce or by themselves.

s1e6

CHOCOLATE PRALINE COOKIES

CONTRIBUTED BY ARIANNA TZOUNAKOS

SOOKIE'S KITCHEN

For Lorelai's engagement to Max, Sookie decides to throw her a party. Whether you call it an engagement party or call it a wedding shower, for Sookie all that matters is figuring out which cookie she will serve.

This is one of the two contestants—the chocolate praline cookie. Enjoy a true Gilmore moment by making these and the coconut macaroons, then host a taste test. Odds are, you'll get the same results as Sookie did—they'll both win.

For praline topping:

½ c	Almonds, hazelnuts, or pecans
½ c	Sugar
2 T	Water
1 T	Unsalted butter
6 oz.	Melting chocolate
½ c	Heavy whipping cream

For chocolate heart cookies:

1 c	Flour
¾ c	Cocoa powder
1½ t	Baking powder
⅛ t	Salt
4 oz.	Melting chocolate
½ c	Unsalted butter, room temperature
1 ¼ c	Sugar
1	Egg

To make praline topping:

Prepare oven and pans: Preheat oven to 350°F. Place parchment paper or a baking mat on a baking sheet. Cover a second baking sheet with wax paper. Set aside.

Toast nuts: Place nuts in a single layer on top of the parchment/silicone mat-covered pan. Place pan in oven. Toast nuts for 7 minutes. Remove from oven and set aside. Keep oven heated to 350°F.

Make pralines: Combine sugar and water in a medium saucepan. Bring to a boil over medium heat and allow to caramelize. Once the mixture reaches a light brown color, stir in butter and nuts. Make sure nuts are evenly coated. Spread praline mixture onto the wax paper–lined baking sheet. Let pralines cool for 15–20 minutes.

Grind pralines: Once the pralines have cooled, break them into quarter-sized pieces for the food processor. Grind the pieces in the food processor until they turn into a fine, bread-crumb-like consistency. Set aside.

Melt chocolate: In a double boiler over medium heat, melt down chocolate. Add praline mixture to chocolate and stir well. Remove from heat.

Make praline chocolate: Heat heavy cream in a medium saucepan over medium heat. Once heavy cream begins to simmer, add chocolate praline mixture and mix well. Once praline chocolate is fully mixed and thickened, pour mixture onto the wax paper–lined baking sheet and leave refrigerated until cookies are ready.

To make chocolate, heart-shaped cookies:
Mix dry ingredients: In a medium mixing bowl, combine flour, cocoa powder, baking powder, and salt. Set aside.

Melt chocolate: In a double boiler over medium heat, melt down chocolate. Allow 5 minutes for chocolate to cool.

Mix wet ingredients: In a large mixing bowl, add butter and sugar. Using an electric hand mixer, beat together until fully combined and creamy. Add melted chocolate. Beat to combine. Add egg. Beat to combine.

Make cookie dough: One cup at a time, add dry mixture to wet ingredients until all dry ingredients have been incorporated into dough.

Refrigerate dough: Remove cookie dough from bowl, wrap in plastic wrap, and place in the refrigerator for about 1 hour.

Bake cookies: Roll out cookie dough to half an inch thick and use a heart-shaped cookie cutter to cut out cookies. Place hearts on baking sheet and put in the oven. Bake for 15 minutes. Remove from oven and let cool 5 minutes. Move cookies to cooling rack.

Add praline chocolate: Allow cookies to cool completely. Then use a small spatula, a spreader, or a butter knife to spread the praline mixture onto the cookie. Serve.

Makes 12 cookies.

COCONUT MACAROONS

SOOKIE'S KITCHEN

Along with the chocolate praline cookies, these coconut macaroons are the cookies Sookie chose to serve at the party celebrating Lorelai's engagement to Max.

When you make these, they don't have to be heart-shaped. They can easily be round, or oval, or shaped like a Jeep being driven by a runaway bride.

2½ c	Shredded coconut, sweetened
¾ c	Sugar
5 T	Flour
¼ t	Salt
4	Large egg whites
1 t	Vanilla extract
1 c	White chocolate chips
¼ c	Heavy cream

Prepare pan and oven: Set out a cookie sheet topped with a silicone mat or parchment paper. Set aside. Place rack in center position of oven. Preheat oven to 325°F.

Mix dry ingredients: In large mixing bowl, combine coconut, sugar, flour, and salt. Mix thoroughly with a fork. Set aside.

Beat egg whites: Place egg whites in a separate large mixing bowl. Add vanilla. Use an electric hand mixer to beat the eggs on high speed until stiff peaks form. Turn off mixer. Using a silicone spatula or wooden spoon, fold egg whites into dry mixture until fully combined.

Bake cookies: Cookies may be shaped with cookie cutters or dropped onto the pan in small mounds. If shaping, make cookies ½-inch thick. If dropping, form into a mound 2 inches in diameter by 1 inch tall. Place pan in oven and bake for 20–25 minutes. Once the pan has been in the oven 15 minutes, begin checking the cookies every few minutes. When they begin to turn golden brown around the outer edges, cook for 5–7 minutes longer. Remove pan from oven. Let cool for 10 minutes. Use a spatula to slowly, gently move cookies from pan onto a cooling rack.

Make glaze: Pour white chocolate chips into a heat-proof medium mixing bowl. Bring heavy cream to a boil in a saucepan over medium-high heat. Pour cream over chocolate chips. Let stand 5–7 minutes. Whisk chocolate until it is smooth with no lumps. If lumps persist, heat bowl in oven for 1 minute. Remove, and continue whisking until smooth. Add ½ drop to 1 drop food coloring, if desired. Let cool at room temperature for 10–15 minutes.

Glaze cookies: Drizzle glaze onto shaped cookies. Turn drop cookie upside down and dip in glaze, then return cookie to drying rack or plate. Serve.

Makes 14–16 heart-shaped cookies.

Tester—Ashley Scarborough

HOMEMADE MALLOMARS®

Can you pinpoint the exact day you first heard of this magical cookie called a "Mallomar"? The first time you ever knew such a wonderful thing existed? Quite possibly, it was Tuesday, April 22, 2003, sometime between 8 and 9 p.m. This is when this episode of *Gilmore Girls* first aired—Lorelai's 35th birthday. Rory meticulously arranges the cookies on their kitchen table to spell out "Happy Birthday" to her mother.

One fun twist on the episode: it's called, "Happy Birthday, Baby," episode 18 from season 3, or 3:18. In real life, Lauren Graham's birthday is March 18, or 3/18.

Amy Sherman-Palladino thinks of everything.

For the wafers:

1 c	**All-purpose flour**
1 c	**Whole wheat flour**
½ c	**Sugar**
½ t	**Baking soda**
¼ t	**Salt**
½ c	**Butter**
¼ c	**Water**

For the marshmallow filling:

3 T	**Gelatin, unflavored**
1½ c	**Water,** *divided*
1 c	**Corn syrup, light**
½ c	**Sugar**

For the chocolate coating:

1 c	**Bittersweet chocolate chips**
1 c	**Milk chocolate chips**
1 t	**Coconut oil**

Prep oven and pan: Place oven rack in the center position. Preheat oven to 375°F. Prepare baking sheet by covering it with parchment paper. Set aside.

Mix dry ingredients: In a medium size mixing bowl, mix flours, sugar, baking soda, and salt.

Brown butter: Place butter in small saucepan over medium heat. Once butter melts, let it continue to cook until it turns a medium caramel brown. Butter will foam. Once the foam begins to disappear, the butter will be the correct color. Remove from heat.

Make dough: Add browned butter to dry ingredients. Mix with a fork until the butter is fully absorbed and evenly distributed. Add water. Again, mix with fork until water is fully absorbed and evenly distributed. At this point, the dough will still look dry and crumbly. Either with a fork or with your hands, press the mixture into a ball, or into large chunks.

Roll and cut dough: Place a large piece of wax paper on a dry, flat surface. Turn the dough out onto the wax paper. Cover dough with a second large sheet of wax paper. Use a rolling pin to roll the dough until it is flat and roughly ¼–½ inch thick. Remove the top sheet of wax paper. Use a cookie cutter, small glass, shot glass, or jigger to cut the dough into small circles. Each circle should be roughly 1½–2 inches in diameter. Use a spatula or fork to gently remove the circles from the bottom sheet of wax paper. Place each circle onto the prepared baking sheet, spaced roughly an inch apart.

Bake the dough: Place the baking sheet in the oven, on the center rack. Bake for 12 minutes. Remove from oven. Set aside to cool for 10 minutes. Using a spatula, remove each cookie/cracker and place onto a wire rack to cool fully.

Bloom gelatin: In a large mixing bowl, sprinkle gelatin. Pour in ½ cup of water. Don't stir. But do move the water around until all of the gelatin is covered. Set aside.

Prepare mixer: Set up a hand mixer next to the bowl with the gelatin—plug it in and insert the beaters. There won't be time to set this up later.

Make syrup: In a Dutch oven or large saucepan, add corn syrup, sugar, and 1 cup water. Stir. Turn on the heat to high. Continue to heat, stirring occasionally, until the temperature reaches 240°F (soft ball stage). Remove from heat immediately. (Don't allow the syrup to get any hotter than 240°F).

Make marshmallow: Pour a small amount of the hot syrup into the gelatin mixture. Using the hand mixer on a low speed, gently mix the two. Gradually pour the remainder of the syrup into the gelatin, increasing the speed of your mixer as you go. By the time all of the syrup has been poured into the bowl, the mixer should be on its highest speed. Continue to mix for roughly 6 minutes. At first, mixture will have a loose, liquid consistency and its color will be light yellow. As you continue to mix, the mixture will become more firm and gooey and will turn a bright, shiny white. Once the mixture begins to pull away from the sides of the bowl to form a ball in the center of the bowl, stop mixing. Your marshmallow is done.

Continued on the next page . . .

Tester—Emilia Hald

Eat Like a Gilmore DAILY CRAVINGS

Top the wafers: Using a tablespoon or a cookie scoop or a pastry bag, place a dollop of marshmallow on top of each wafer. Use as much marshmallow as you like. I prefer about the size of a ping pong ball. This will get messy! Allow the marshmallow-topped wafers to sit for roughly an hour while the marshmallow sets.

Melt chocolate: Set a double boiler on the stove. (If you don't have a double boiler, place 1–2 inches of water in a small saucepan and place a metal bowl or heat-resistant glass bowl or smaller saucepan inside, so the water is touching the bottom, but not overflowing.) Place both chocolates and the coconut oil in the top bowl/pan. Over medium-high heat, allow the water to heat and begin to melt the chocolate. Wait to stir until you see most of the bottom chocolate has started to melt. Using a spatula or spoon, gently stir the chocolate to move the unmelted chocolate to the bottom. (Take care not to get any water in the chocolate as this will cause it to seize up into a firm ball.) Once all of the chocolate has melted and is smooth, remove from heat.

Cover cookies: One at a time, place each cookie into the chocolate, marshmallow side first. Use a fork to gently turn the cookie in the chocolate, so the bottom gets coated. Once all sides of the cookie are coated, use the fork to remove it from the chocolate and place it on a wire rack. Repeat for each cookie. If you'd like to add sprinkles to your cookies, do this now, while the chocolate is still "wet."

Set and serve: Allow cookies to "air dry" until the chocolate is firm to the touch. These are your homemade Mallomars! Serve and enjoy.

Makes approximately 24 Mallomars.

SUGAR COOKIES WITH ICING

Rory's return from London marks the beginning of a late Christmas season at Lorelai and Christopher's house. The house is decorated with multiple deeply discounted Christmas trees, and new stockings Christopher bought hang from the bannister. Lorelai, Rory, and Gigi make cranberry and popcorn garlands while wearing festive sweaters, and Christopher, Rory, and Gigi decorate the freshly baked cookies. It's the perfect picture of festive domesticity.

This episode is our only opportunity to see a full Gilmore-style Christmas scene. Sure, in prior episodes we see Santa burgers and watch as the townspeople assemble the annual nativity scene. But this episode is the only one fully immersed in holiday spirit.

Immerse yourself in the holiday spirit, any holiday, with these cookies. Cut them into any shape you choose. They make great cookies for Valentine's Day, St. Patrick's Day, Arbor Day . . . or simply cut them into the letter "G" and celebrate a day of binge-watching *Gilmore Girls*.

For cookies:

Note: Dough requires overnight refrigeration

5 c	Flour, plus more for dusting
1 t	Baking powder
1 t	Baking soda
1 t	Salt
1 t	Ground nutmeg
1 c	Butter, softened
2 c	Sugar
2	Eggs
1 c	Sour cream
1 t	Vanilla

For icing:

2 c	Powdered sugar
1 T	Milk
1–2 T	Corn syrup
½ t	Vanilla extract

Mix dry ingredients: In a medium mixing bowl, combine flour, baking powder, baking soda, salt, and nutmeg. Set aside.

Mix wet ingredients: Place butter in a large mixing bowl. Add sugar. Using an electric hand mixer, beat the two together until smooth and creamy. Add the eggs one at a time, mixing after each. Add sour cream and vanilla. Mix until fully combined and smooth. Scrape down the sides of the bowl using a silicone spatula.

Add dry ingredients: Gradually add the dry ingredients to the wet ingredients, mixing the dough as you go. Once all dry ingredients have been added in, ensure dough is evenly mixed.

Refrigerate dough: Roll out plastic wrap or aluminum foil onto a flat work surface. Turn dough out onto the plastic or foil. Wrap dough completely so no air can get to it. Refrigerate dough overnight (6 hours minimum).

Prepare pans and oven: Set out two cookie sheets covered in parchment paper or silicone baking mats. Set aside. Ensure oven rack is positioned in the center of oven. Preheat oven to 350°F.

Cut out dough: Cover a flat work surface with a thin layer of flour. Place half of dough on the flour. Gently flatten it with your palm, then sprinkle the dough with flour. Use a rolling pin to roll dough out until it is about ½ inch thick. Use cookie cutters to cut dough into desired shapes. As you cut, remove the cookie from the cutter and place it on one of the prepared pans. Repeat for all of the dough. When no more cookies can be cut from rolled dough, gather all the dough together into a ball, add more "fresh" dough to it, and roll it out again. Continue until all dough has been cut.

Bake cookies: Once the first pan is full of cut dough, place the pan in the oven. Bake for 12–15 minutes. Watch for the edges to turn a light brown. The center of the cookie should still be a light cream color (not brown). Remove pan from oven. Let cookies cool for 5 minutes. Then move them to a cooling rack. Repeat for all cookies.

Make icing: In a medium bowl, mix together powdered sugar, milk, 1 tablespoon corn syrup, and vanilla. If consistency is too thick, add additional corn syrup. Mix in food coloring, as desired (white icing may be separated into multiple small bowls in order to make various colors).

Decorate cookies: Brush icing onto cookies using a cookie decorating brush (a clean, new/unused make-up brush will work). Allow decorated cookies to sit for 15 minutes to harden. Serve.

Makes 20–24 cookies.

s7e11

MERINGUE COOKIES

SOOKIE'S KITCHEN

After some persuading from her mother, Rory agrees to go out for dinner with Trevor, the handsomely bland guy from one of her classes at Yale. During the date, she tells a riveting "urine mints" anecdote, during which she must have been thinking, "the counselor at Chilton was right . . . I really do lack social skills!" Finally, the date ends. Feeling like a dating failure, Rory drives home to Stars Hollow. Luke is over for a movie night and has fallen asleep on the sofa. So, the Gilmore girls head into the kitchen. Out of the cabinet Lorelai produces a sealed container filled with meringue cookies. The girls sit at the table, eating cookies and talking about dating.

This recipe is attributed to Sookie. There's really no way to know for sure who made these cookies. But we do know for sure who didn't make them: Lorelai. They definitely look homemade, though. So Sookie seems like the safest bet.

The next time you need to sit at the kitchen table and have serious discussions about life, go with your gut and make a batch of these light, guilt-free cookies. Just make sure everyone has washed their hands before eating them!

5 oz	Egg whites (about 4 large eggs)
1 t	Vanilla extract
⅛ t	Cream of tartar
Pinch	Salt
10 oz	Superfine sugar (about 1½ cups)

Prep oven and baking sheets: Preheat oven to 225°F. Cover two baking sheets with parchment paper or silicone baking mats. Set aside.

Mix ingredients: In medium mixing bowl, add egg whites, vanilla extract, cream of tartar, and salt. Beat on high speed with hand mixer until egg whites begin to form stiff peaks. Gradually add sugar. Once all sugar has been added, continue to beat on high speed for 3–5 minutes. This will help the sugar dissolve into the egg white mixture.

Pipe cookies onto baking sheets: Prepare a piping bag with a decorative tip of your choosing (a #1M tip was used to make the cookies pictured). Scoop the batter in batches into the piping bag. Pipe batter into cookies 1½–2 inches wide by ¾–1 inch tall.

Bake cookies: Place baking sheets in oven. Bake for 45 minutes. Remove from oven. Let cool 10 minutes. Serve.

Store cookies: Place additional cookies in airtight container.

Makes 30 cookies.

Note: Peach sweater in photo provided by Gilmore Garbs, the place for all Gilmore-related clothing. www.gilmoregarbs.com

s4 e5

MARZIPAN

A sparkling change from Emily and Richard's usual condescending—albeit witty and humorous—remarks, the elder Gilmores' enthusiasm for a dessert straight from the cloistered nuns of France makes this treat even more unique than plutonium. Although the exact appeal of marzipan is as confounding to Lorelei as the plural form of cul-de-sac, even Lorelei can't resist when the confection is shaped like a cute little bunny. However, in Lorelei's case, the dessert serves a greater purpose: the chance to subtly flirt with her latest love interest, Jason Stiles.

You won't need Jason or Emily to enjoy this sugary treat, regardless of whether you choose the one shaped like a pig, or a bunny. With this recipe you can impress all your friends with your world culture and culinary prowess. Just keep some napkins handy in case your friends' taste buds are more in line with Lorelai and Rory.

1¼ c	**Almond meal (without almond skins)**
1¼ c	**Powdered sugar**
Pinch	**Salt**
1½ t	**Almond extract**
¼ t	**Vanilla extract**
1	**Egg white**

Mix marzipan: In a medium mixing bowl, combine almond meal, powdered sugar, and salt. Mix until fully combined. Add extracts and egg white. Mix using a hand mixer (a food processor may also be used). The result will be marzipan.

To store: wrap tightly in plastic wrap and refrigerate.

To make colored marzipan: Select the amount of marzipan you'd like to color. Begin by using a very small amount of color and add more as desired. Place marzipan onto a piece of plastic wrap or wax paper. Into a teaspoon, squeeze one drop of food coloring. Dip a toothpick or fork tine into the food coloring and then onto the marzipan. With your hands, begin to work the color into the marzipan. Once the marzipan is an even color, decide whether or not to add more color. Repeat until it's the color you desire.

Makes 2½ cups of marzipan.

Warning: this recipe contains raw egg, which may be harmful to health.

To watch the how-to video Kristi used to create this pig and bunny, please visit http://www.eatlikeagilmore.com

s4 e10

Intro by Lisa Larson

Tester—Lauren Cutrone

PEANUT BRITTLE

TOWN FAVORITE

While Dean's busy working with Tom on construction of the Dragonfly, Lindsey spends her days in the kitchen with her mom, making treats to bring the guys—including peanut brittle hard enough to break some teeth. Isn't this exactly the type of wife Dean said he wanted? The traditional homemaker who stays at home, Donna Reed-ing it, while the husband is out earning money for the family? He got what he wanted. So why is he still so hung up on Rory?

This peanut brittle is light and easy to eat. Plus, you won't have to spend a full day in the kitchen making it.

1 lb	Unsalted peanuts, shells and skins removed
4 T	Butter, plus more for greasing pans
1½ t	Baking soda
2 t	Vanilla
1 ½ c	Sugar
1 c	Water
1 c	Light corn syrup

Prepare pans: Set out two baking sheets and grease them with butter. Set aside.

Prepare ingredients: Measure out peanuts, butter, baking soda, and vanilla. You'll need quick access to these. Set aside.

Heat syrup: In a Dutch oven, stockpot, or large saucepan, add sugar, water, and corn syrup. Gently stir a few times to combine. Insert candy thermometer into pan. Over high heat, without stirring, bring mixture to 240°F. Add peanuts and stir to combine.

Heat syrup to hard crack: Continue to heat mixture over high heat, stirring every 30 seconds or so to prevent burning; especially at 260°F and higher. Once mixture reaches 300°F, quickly but carefully, add butter, baking soda, and vanilla. Stir quickly to combine.

Spread peanut brittle: Using oven mitts to hold the sides of the pan, moving quickly, carry the pan to the baking sheets. Scoop out half the mixture onto each sheet. Use a silicone spatula to spread the mixture into a thin, flat, even layer. Repeat this step for pan #2. Allow peanut brittle to set at room temperature for 30 minutes.

Serve: Break peanut brittle into pieces.

Makes 20–30 pieces of brittle.

Tester—Katlyn & Teri

FUDGE

We often hear about other townspeople we don't get to see on screen—Harry, the Twinkle Lights shop owner, or Stan, the townsman who left money in his will to restore the church bells. However, we don't typically hear about people who lived in the town in the past.

One exception is the story we hear during one town meeting of the Fudge Queen, Margie. She was the homewrecker who wooed the candy shop owner, Art, away from his girlfriend, Fay, who owned the flower shop.

So, in honor of Margie, and all of the Stars Hollow homewreckers who came before her, here is a recipe to make some fudge.

¼ c	Butter
2 t	Vanilla
3 c	Sugar
6 oz	Unsweetened cocoa
¼ t	Salt
1½ c	Whole milk
1 c	Mini marshmallows, mini chocolate chips, or chopped nuts, *optional*

Prep pan: Line an 8x8-inch pan with aluminum foil so it covers the bottom and all four sides of pan. Set aside.

Prep butter and vanilla: Measure out butter and vanilla. Place them in ramekins or small bowls near the stove for easy access.

Make fudge: Combine sugar, cocoa, salt, and milk in large saucepan or Dutch oven. Don't mix. Insert a candy thermometer into pot. Turn on high heat. Once ingredients begin to melt, use a silicone spatula or wooden spoon to slowly combine them, taking care not to get sugar or cocoa on the side of the pan. Heat mixture until it reaches soft ball stage, 235°F. Add butter and vanilla. Stir vigorously (but carefully!) until combined. Continue to stir until the mixture has cooled. Let mixture sit in pan for 15 minutes, cooling. Stir vigorously again for 2–3 minutes. Add any mix-in ingredients and stir. Pour fudge into prepared pan. Let cool at room temperature for 4 hours.

Serve fudge: Remove from pan. Remove foil. Cut into 1 inch x 2 inch rectangles. Serve.

Makes 32 pieces.

s5 e3

Tester—Hannah Faber

CARAMEL APPLES

For Halloween, Lorelai hangs caramel apples from her tree. What's the point of this tradition? Does Lorelai make the caramel herself? How does she get the apples onto the tree? Are the kids supposed to jump up and get a caramel apple?

So many questions.

These make a fun fall treat—any time during the fall, not just on Halloween. In fact, don't make them for Halloween. Do the sausage thing—it's way more exciting.

24	Apples (Granny Smith recommended)
24	Wooden sticks
1 c	Sugar
1 c	Brown sugar
¼ c	Light corn syrup
1 c	Water
½ c	Butter
2 c	Heavy cream
¼ c	Vanilla extract

Prepare apples: Wash and dry apples. Remove stems. Set each apple upright and insert stick halfway into apple core so stick stands upright. Set aside. Near the stove, cover a flat surface (a tray, cutting board, countertop, etc.) with wax paper.

Make caramel: In stockpot or Dutch oven, combine sugars, corn syrup, and water. Do not stir. Turn on heat to high. Insert candy thermometer into pot. Once ingredients begin to melt, use a wooden spoon or a silicone spatula to gently stir two or three times, taking care not to get sugar on the sides of the pot. Once temperature hits 255°F, add butter and heavy cream. Stir gently (and carefully!). Bring temperature up to 240°F. Stir in vanilla. Remove from heat. Let cool 7–8 minutes (not more!).

Dip apples: One by one, dip each apple in the caramel, moving briskly. Ensure apple is coated with caramel on all sides. Hold apple above pan for a few moments allowing for extra caramel to drip off. Stand apple up on the wax paper. Repeat for all apples. Allow caramel on apples to harden. Serve.

Makes 24 apples.

Tester—Hannah Faber

Eat Like a Gilmore DAILY CRAVINGS

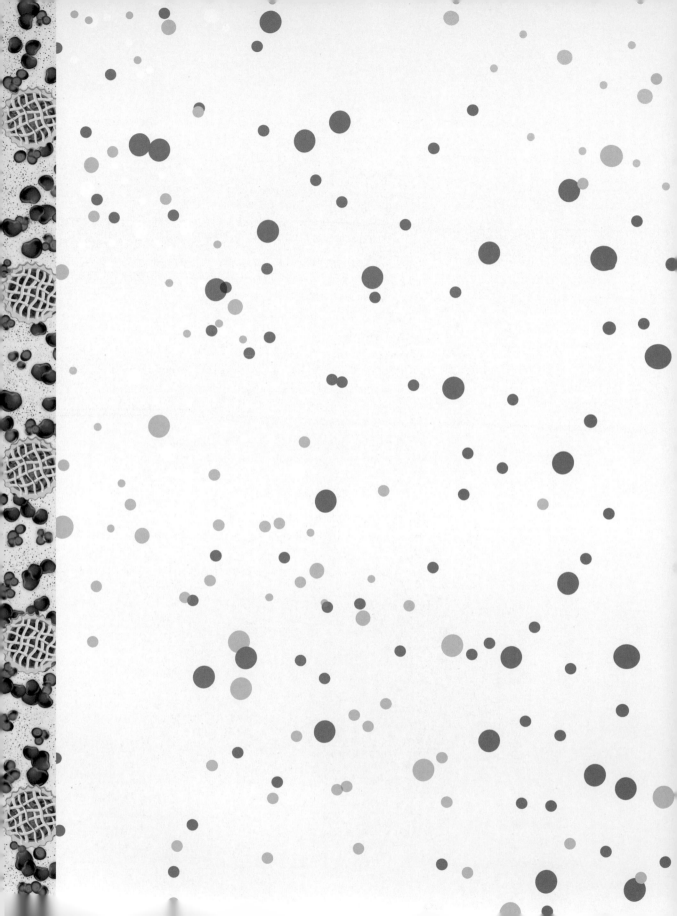

Pies & Things

APPLE PANDOWDY

WESTON'S BAKERY

It makes sense this would be served at Weston's, because it is a throwback to the 1950s. If you're looking for a fresh, yet old-fashioned take on apple pie, try this!

For filling:

6	Apples, peeled, sliced, Granny Smith recommended
½ c	Sugar
½ c	Brown sugar
1½ T	Lemon juice, freshly squeezed
1½ t	Ground cinnamon
½ t	Ground cloves
½ t	Ground nutmeg
2 T	Cornstarch
4 T	Butter
	Vanilla ice cream, for serving, *optional*

For crust:

1 c	Flour
½ t	Salt
3 T	Cold shortening
¼ c	Cold butter
¼ c	Ice water
	Milk, for brushing
	Coarse sugar

Masticate apples: In a large bowl combine apples, sugars, and lemon juice. Gently mix until most apples are coated with sugar. Let stand at room temperature 1 hour.

Make piecrust dough: In a medium mixing bowl, combine flour and salt. Add shortening and butter. Use a pastry cutter or dough cutter to cut the fats into the flour until the flour looks like little white peas. Add half of the water and continue to cut/mix dough using cutter. A dough will begin to form. If the dough seems dry or if substantial flour remains at the bottom of the bowl, add additional tablespoons of water as needed. Roll dough into a ball. Press ball into a flat disc. Wrap in plastic wrap and refrigerate for 30 minutes.

Prepare pans and oven: Cover a baking sheet with parchment paper or a silicone baking mat. Set out a 2-quart baking dish. Put the oven rack in the middle position. Preheat oven to 375°F.

Roll out dough: Generously flour a flat work surface. Remove dough from refrigerator. Use a rolling pin to roll dough into a 10–11-inch square. Use a large, sharp knife or a pizza cutter to cut the dough into long strips, about 1½ inches wide. Place dough strips on baking sheet. Brush each strip with milk. Sprinkle coarse sugar onto each strip.

Bake dough: Place pan in oven and bake for 10 minutes. Remove from oven and let cool.

Make filling: Use slotted spoon to transfer apples into a large saucepan or Dutch oven and add cinnamon, cloves, and nutmeg. Add cornstarch to juices remaining in bowl. Stir to combine. Add juices to pot. Cook over medium heat for 10 minutes. Use a slotted spoon to remove apples from pot, placing them in the baking dish.

Thicken filling: Heat juices over medium heat, stirring often until they begin to thicken. Add butter and stir until fully melted and combined. Remove from heat.

Assemble: Place dough strips over the apple filling in a single layer so top is covered. Pour sauce over dough strips. Gently press down dough so it becomes partially submerged in juice.

Bake: Place baking dish in oven. Bake for 20 minutes. Remove from oven. Let cool 15 minutes. Cut and serve with vanilla ice cream.

s3 e10

Tester—Andrea Blatt

BOSTON CREAM PIE

CONTRIBUTED BY BY ANNEMARIE CONTE

There are two ways to do Boston Cream Pie: the down-and-dirty Lorelai way using premade, store-bought ingredients or the Emily way. For Emily Gilmore, you must have your cook hand-stir the pastry cream or it isn't worth it. Plus, she would definitely know the history of Boston cream pie, that it all started at the Omni Parker House Hotel in Boston (the same place that invented Parker House Rolls).

The trick to this is to have cake which is sturdy enough to handle the center layer of cream, but not too stiff and tough. The key is to make sure you're working quickly to get the cake in the oven once you've added the hot milk mixture.

This recipe makes extra pastry cream, because if you don't serve the cake immediately, it tends to soak up a bunch of the cream. This recipe offers enough to make it feel like you are getting your money's worth.

For pastry cream:

2 T	Butter
1 t	Vanilla extract
2 c	Whole milk (or a combo of cream and milk)
1 c	Sugar, *divided*
Pinch	Salt
3 T	Cornstarch
4	Egg yolks

For cake:

1½ c	Flour
1½ t	Baking powder
¾ t	Salt
¾ c	Milk
6 T	Unsalted butter
3 lg	Eggs
1 c	Sugar
1 t	Vanilla extract

For glaze:

5 oz	Dark chocolate
¼ c	Heavy cream
1 T	Corn syrup

Pastry cream (make at least 4 hours ahead)

Prepare ingredients: Prepare butter and vanilla in small bowls or ramekins. Set aside. In a medium saucepan, over medium-high heat, boil together milk, ½ cup sugar, and the pinch of salt. In a small bowl, whisk together ½ cup sugar, cornstarch, and yolks.

Temper the eggs: Stirring constantly, slowly trickle the hot milk mixture into the egg mixture.

Make pastry cream: Pour tempered mixture back into the pot and cook on medium, stirring constantly, until it thickens. Take the pot off the heat (strain through a fine-mesh sieve, if necessary) and add butter and vanilla. Stir until melted.

Refrigerate pastry cream: Pour the hot pastry cream into a glass bowl and press a piece of plastic wrap against the top of the cream to prevent a skin from forming. Refrigerate until cold, about 3 hours or up to 3 days.

Make cake:

Stir together flour, baking powder, and salt. Set aside.

Combine milk and butter in a small pot. Set over low heat.

In the bowl of a stand mixer with a whisk attachment, whisk together eggs and sugar on medium until mixture is thick and falls in thick ribbons from the whisk (about 5 minutes). Beat in vanilla.

Stir in dry ingredients until combined.

Gently drizzle in hot milk mixture. Stir to combine.

Immediately divide between two 9-inch round cake pans (or pour into a single 9-inch round cake pan).

Bake at 325°F for 20 minutes (or for 40–42 minutes if using only one pan).

Cool cakes in pan for 10 minutes.

If using one pan, slice cake in half to create two small rounds.

Make glaze: Combine dark chocolate, heavy cream, and corn syrup in a double boiler or a small bowl set over a simmering pot. Stir until melted.

Assemble cake: Spread pastry cream between two cake rounds. Gently pour glaze on top, pushing glaze to the edge so it drips down the sides of the cake.

PIECRUST

TOWN FAVORITE

When Rory visits the home of a Harvard alumnus, she learns far more than she was planning. Oh sure, she gets some good information from the alumnus, himself. But it's the impromptu conversation she has with the "lost" daughter, Carol, that makes the biggest impression on her. From learning about the college conveyor belt to straight, shiny, Harvard hair, Rory gets a bunny-sized earful. She also hears Carol use an insult she likely hadn't heard before when Carol referred to her manager as a "piecrust".

To set the record straight, "piecrust" is not an insult. Piecrust is flaky, buttery goodness. It also provides the vehicle for pie filling. What could be more important?

Double crust 9-inch:

2 c	Flour
1 t	Salt
⅓ c	Cold shortening
½ c	Cold butter
½ c	Ice water
	Coarse sugar

Single Crust 9-inch:

1 c	Flour
½ t	Salt
3 T	Cold shortening
¼ c	Cold butter
2 T	Ice water

Prepare pie plate and oven: Set out a 9-inch pie plate. Ensure the oven rack is in the middle position. Preheat oven to 400°.

Make piecrust dough: In a medium mixing bowl, combine flour and salt. Add shortening and butter. Use a pastry cutter or dough cutter to cut the fats into the flour until the flour looks like little white peas. Add half of the water and continue to cut/mix dough using cutter. A dough will begin to form. If the dough seems dry or if substantial flour remains at the bottom of the bowl, add additional tablespoons of water as needed. Roll dough into a ball (two equal balls if making double crust). Press ball(s) into a flat disc. Wrap each in plastic wrap and refrigerate for 30 minutes.

Roll out bottom crust: Generously flour a flat work surface. Remove dough from refrigerator. Use a rolling pin to roll dough into an 11–12-inch circle. Place rolling pin onto the dough, toward one side edge. Fold the dough onto the rolling pin, then slowly roll the rolling pin so the dough loosely wraps around it. (If the dough is stuck to the work surface, use a dough cutter to gently scrape the dough off the surface as you go.) Position the rolling pin over the pie plate, then unroll the dough into the pie plate. Press the dough into position, making sure there are no air bubbles under the dough.

Roll out top crust (if using): Roll second crust same as first. After the pie is filled, place the second crust over the top, lining up the edges with the bottom crust. Crimp the edges of top and bottom crusts together using a fork, a crimping tool or your fingers. Cut 10–12 small slits into the top crust evenly around the pie. Sprinkle with coarse sugar. Bake as directed.

s3 e3

APPLE PIE

Jess is making money, but Luke doesn't know how or where. After Luke asks Jess if he's a gigolo, Jess confesses. He has a job as a forklift operator at Walmart.

While Luke gets a few laughs and jabs in about Walmart, Jess is sitting at Luke's table, the one covered with the cerulean tablecloth, eating the apple pie Luke brought upstairs from the diner. All of a sudden Luke realizes, Jess is eating apple pie and working at Walmart. He's the All-American boy.

For filling:

8 c	Peeled, cored, and sliced apples (Granny Smith recommended)
1½ c	Sugar
2 t	Cinnamon
¼ t	Ground nutmeg
⅛ t	Ground allspice
2 T	Lemon juice, freshly squeezed
¼ c	Cornstarch
2 T	Butter

For crust:

2 c	Flour
1 t	Salt
⅓ c	Cold shortening
½ c	Cold butter
½ c	Ice water
	Coarse sugar

Macerate apples: Place apple slices in a large mixing bowl. Measure sugar into a medium bowl and add spices. Mix together. Top apples with lemon juice and gently turn apple slices until lemon juice is distributed. Pour sugar mixture on top of apples. Gently turn apples to distribute sugar. Let sit for 60–90 minutes.

Prepare pie plate and oven: Set out a 9-inch pie plate. Ensure the oven rack is in the middle position. Preheat oven to 400°F.

Make piecrust dough: In a medium mixing bowl, combine flour and salt. Add shortening and butter. Use a pastry cutter or dough cutter to cut the fats into the flour, until the flour looks like little white peas. Add 2 tablespoons of water and continue to cut/mix dough using cutter. A dough will begin to form. If the dough seems dry or if substantial flour remains at the bottom of the bowl, add 1 or 2 additional tablespoons of water as needed. Roll dough into two even balls. Press each ball into a flat disc. Wrap each in plastic wrap and refrigerate for 30 minutes.

Roll out dough: Generously flour a flat work surface. Remove one disc of dough from refrigerator. Use a rolling pin to roll dough into an 11–12-inch circle. Place rolling pin onto the dough, toward one side edge. Fold the dough onto the rolling pin, then slowly roll the rolling pin so the dough loosely wraps around it. (If the dough is stuck to the work surface, use a dough cutter to gently scrape the dough off the surface as you go.) Position the rolling pin over the pie plate, then unroll the dough into the pie plate. Press the dough into position, making sure there are no air bubbles under the dough. Repeat with the second disc of dough, leaving it on the work surface.

Make pie: Using a slotted spoon, spoon apple slices out of bowl, leaving juice in bowl. Place apple slices in bottom piecrust, distributing them evenly. Using a fork, mix cornstarch into juice left in bowl. (Juice will need to be cold for this to work, so be sure not to heat it.) Continue to mix until cornstarch is fully dissolved. Pour juice over apples in pie. Dot apples with butter.

Working quickly, top the pie with second crust. Crimp edges and trim any excess dough. Cut 10–12 small slits in top crust. Top with coarse sugar.

Bake pie: Place in oven and bake for 45–50 minutes. Remove from oven. Let cool for 4 hours. Cut and serve.

Tester—Cathi Kennedy

Eat Like a Gilmore DAILY CRAVINGS

PUMPKIN PIE

LUKE'S DINER

Luke heads over to have a movie night with Lorelai and, not knowing the drill, brings food: a bunch of burgers, loads of fries, and half a pumpkin pie. When he walks in, he finds Lorelai has already ordered Chinese food and bought beer. True to form, Luke gets concerned that they have too much food. Unphased, Lorelai reassures Luke that there's no such thing. Then they hunker down to watch *Casablanca*.

Meanwhile, what's with the half pie? That's no way to get a Gilmore's attention. Bring a whole pie! Especially if it's pumpkin.

For crust:

1 c	Flour
½ t	Salt
2 T	Cold shortening
4 T	Cold butter
¼ c	Ice water

For filling:

15 oz	Canned pumpkin
12 oz	Canned evaporated milk
¾ c	Brown sugar
2	Eggs
1 T	Ground cinnamon
½ t	Salt
½ t	Ground nutmeg
⅛ t	Ground cloves
⅛ t	Ground allspice

Prepare pie plate and oven: Set out a 9-inch pie plate. Ensure the oven rack is in the middle position. Preheat oven to 375°F.

Make piecrust dough: In a medium mixing bowl, combine flour and salt. Add shortening and butter. Use a pastry cutter or dough cutter to cut the fats into the flour, until the flour looks like little white peas. Add 2 tablespoons of water and continue to cut/mix dough using cutter. A dough will begin to form. If the dough seems dry or if substantial flour remains at the bottom of the bowl, add 1 or 2 additional tablespoons of water as needed. Roll dough into a ball. Press ball into a flat disc. Wrap disc in plastic wrap and refrigerate for 30 minutes.

Roll out dough: Generously flour a flat work surface. Remove dough from refrigerator. Use a rolling pin to roll dough into an 11–12-inch circle. Place rolling pin onto the dough, toward one side edge. Fold the dough onto the rolling pin, then slowly roll the rolling pin so the dough loosely wraps around it. (If the dough is stuck to the work surface, use a dough cutter to gently scrape the dough off the surface as you go.) Position the rolling pin over the pie plate, then unroll the dough into the pie plate. Press the dough into position, making sure there are no air bubbles under the dough. Trim and crimp edges using a crimping tool, a fork, or your fingers.

Bake crust: Add pie weights, pie beads, or a flat foil packet filled with dry beans to the center of the crust. Place pie plate in center of oven and bake for 10 minutes. Remove from oven. Remove weights. Let cool for 10 minutes.

Mix filling: In a large saucepan over low heat, combine pumpkin, milk, and brown sugar. Whisk in eggs one at a time and continue whisking until fully blended after each egg. Add spices and whisk. Remove from heat.

Make pie: Pour filling into par-baked pie shell. Place pie in oven and bake for 25–30 minutes. Watch for the outer edges of the pumpkin filling to begin turning brown. Center of filling may still jiggle slightly. If it is jiggling too much, continue baking for 5 minutes. Remove from oven. Let cool at room temperature for 2 hours. Then serve or refrigerate.

Tester—Rebecca Blanchette

BANANA CREAM PIE

Lorelai comes downstairs to get pie in the middle of the night and finds Logan already there, getting water. The two proceed to have a very open, honest conversation. Logan asks Lorelai, point blank, what about him is worrying her. Lorelai responds from the heart, telling him she worries about his cavalier attitude toward money. Logan responds sincerely, without taking any offense. His reaction reassures Lorelai, so she suggests they sit down and have some pie.

At the time they had three different kinds of pie in the house but, surely, the banana cream pie is the best follow-up to a midnight heart-to-heart talk.

For crust:

1 c	Flour
½ t	Salt
2 T	Cold shortening
4 T	Cold butter
¼ c	Ice water

For filling:

1 T	Butter
1 T	Vanilla
2 c	Cold whole milk
4 T	Cornstarch
3	Egg yolks
¾ c	Sugar
¼ t	Salt
2	Over-ripe bananas, peeled, mashed or pureed, *optional*
4	Bananas, peeled, sliced into small discs

For topping:

2 c	Heavy cream
½ c	Superfine sugar
1 t	Vanilla extract
¼ c	Sour cream
	Vanilla wafer cookies (Nilla wafers recommended)

Prepare pie plate and oven: Set out a 9-inch pie plate. Ensure the oven rack is in the middle position. Preheat oven to 400°F.

Make piecrust dough: In a medium mixing bowl, combine flour and salt. Add shortening and butter. Use a pastry cutter or dough cutter to cut the fats into the flour, until the flour looks like little white peas. Add 2 tablespoons of water and continue to cut/mix dough using cutter. A dough will begin to form. If the dough seems dry or if substantial flour remains at the bottom of the bowl, add 1 or 2 additional tablespoons of water as needed. Roll dough into a ball. Press ball into a flat disc. Wrap disc in plastic wrap and refrigerate for 30 minutes.

Roll out dough: Generously flour a flat work surface. Remove dough from refrigerator. Use a rolling pin to roll dough into an 11–12-inch circle. Place rolling pin onto the dough, toward one side edge. Fold the dough onto the rolling pin, then slowly roll the rolling pin so the dough loosely wraps around it. (If the dough is stuck to the work surface, use a dough cutter to gently scrape the dough off the surface as you go.) Position the rolling pin over the pie plate, then unroll the dough into the pie plate. Press the dough into position, making sure there are no air bubbles under the dough. Trim and crimp edges using a crimping tool, a fork, or your fingers.

Bake crust: Add pie weights, pie beads, or a flat foil packet filled with dry beans to the center of the crust. Place pie plate in center of oven and bake for 30 minutes. Remove from oven. Remove weights. Let cool for 20 minutes.

Prepare butter and vanilla: Measure and set out both butter and vanilla so you can access them in a hurry.

Combine milk and cornstarch: Measure milk, and while it's still in the measuring cup, add cornstarch and gently whisk until the two are fully combined.

Make pudding: In a medium saucepan, combine egg yolks, sugar, and salt. Do not stir. Pour in milk/cornstarch mixture.

Whisk together until smooth. Turn on heat to medium-high setting. Continue stirring while pudding heats. It will thicken right before it boils. Watch for bubbles around the edges—when they appear, it indicates the pudding is about to boil. Turn off heat. Stir in butter and vanilla. While pudding is still warm, stir in the pureed overripe banana until fully blended.

Make pie: Arrange cut pieces of banana in piecrust. Pour warm pudding over the bananas, evenly, so pie is level. Refrigerate for 2 hours.

Make whipped cream topping: In a large mixing bowl, combine heavy cream, sugar, and vanilla extract. With mixer set on medium speed, beat until stiff peaks form. Gently fold in sour cream. Beat on high again until stiff peaks form a second time. Cover bowl with lid or plastic wrap. Chill until ready to serve pie.

Serve pie: Spread a thick layer or pipe decorate dollops of whipped cream topping onto top of pie, covering fully. Garnish with vanilla wafer cookies. Cut pie and serve.

s7 e18

Tester—Hannah Faber

Eat Like a Gilmore DAILY CRAVINGS

CHERRY PIE

The night before Thanksgiving, we find out Lorelai has a usual Wednesday meal—it's a French dip sandwich, extra fries, and a slice of cherry pie. Luke already has it in the works when he sees her walk in. He's busy stuffing turkeys, preparing to serve Thanksgiving meals to countless guests the next day. Yet, he still takes the time to think of Lorelai. How sweet and thoughtful is he? Also, what a great idea to make cherry pie the official pie of Thanksgiving Eve—a new tradition!

For filling:

4 c	Fresh cherries, stems and pits removed
1 c	Sugar
¼ c	Flour
½ t	Almond extract, *optional* (amaretto liqueur may be substituted)
3 T	Butter

For crust:

2 c	Flour
1 t	Salt
⅓ c	Cold shortening
½ c	Cold butter
½ c	Ice water
	Coarse sugar

Prepare cherries: Place cherries into a large mixing bowl. Sprinkle evenly with sugar. Let sit for 3 hours. Using a wooden spoon, gently turn cherries every hour to incorporate the sugar.

Prepare pie plate and oven: Set out a 9-inch pie plate. Ensure the oven rack is in the middle position. Preheat oven to 400°F.

Make piecrust dough: In a medium mixing bowl, combine flour and salt. Add shortening and butter. Use a pastry cutter or dough cutter to cut the fats into the flour until the flour looks like little white peas. Add 2 tablespoons of water and continue to cut/mix dough using cutter. A dough will begin to form. If the dough seems dry or if substantial flour remains at the bottom of the bowl, add 1 or 2 additional tablespoons of water as needed. Roll dough into two even balls. Press each ball into a flat disc. Wrap each in plastic wrap and refrigerate for 30 minutes.

Roll out dough: Generously flour a flat work surface. Remove one disc of dough from refrigerator. Use a rolling pin to roll dough into an 11–12-inch circle. Place rolling pin onto the dough, toward one side edge. Fold the dough onto the rolling pin, then slowly roll the rolling pin so the dough loosely wraps around it. (If the dough is stuck to the work surface, use a dough cutter to gently scrape the dough off the surface as you go.) Position the rolling pin over the pie plate, then unroll the dough into the pie plate. Press the dough into position, making sure there are no air bubbles under the dough. Repeat with the second disc of dough, leaving it on the work surface.

Prepare pie: Sprinkle cherries with flour. Add almond extract, if using. Gently fold flour into cherries. Then slowly pour cherries into pie plate. Dot with several pieces of butter around entire pie. Top with second crust. Crimp edges and trim any excess dough. Cut 10–12 small slits in top crust. Top with coarse sugar.

Bake pie: Place in oven and bake for 45–50 minutes. Remove from oven. Let cool for 4 hours. Cut and serve.

Tester—Gabi Faber

PEACH PIE

LUKE'S DINER

Liz is staying at Luke's and, once TJ arrives in town, she's feeling domestic. So, she takes some food from the diner—a few steaks and a peach pie—to make dinner for TJ and Luke. Suddenly Jess shows up and Liz knows it's a positive sign, showing the men in her life are drawn to her. She is wrong about one thing, though— lots of people eat peach pie!

For filling:

7 c	Peeled, pitted, and sliced peaches
1 c	Sugar
2 t	Ground cardamom
2 T	Lemon juice, freshly squeezed
¼ c	Cornstarch
2 T	Butter

For crust:

2 c	Flour
1 t	Salt
⅓ c	Cold shortening
½ c	Cold butter
½ c	Ice water
	Coarse sugar

Macerate peaches: Place peach slices in a large mixing bowl. Measure sugar into a medium bowl and add cardamom. Mix together. Top peaches with lemon juice and gently turn peach slices until lemon juice is distributed. Pour sugar mixture on top of peaches. Gently turn peaches to distribute sugar. Let sit for 60 minutes.

Prepare pie plate and oven: Set out a 9-inch pie plate. Ensure the oven rack is in the middle position. Preheat oven to 450°F.

Make piecrust dough: In a medium mixing bowl, combine flour and salt. Add shortening and butter. Use a pastry cutter or dough cutter to cut the fats into the flour until the flour looks like little white peas. Add 2 tablespoons of water and continue to cut/mix dough using cutter. A dough will begin to form. If the dough seems dry or if substantial flour remains at the bottom of the bowl, add 1 or 2 additional tablespoons of water as needed. Roll dough into two even balls. Press each ball into a flat disc. Wrap each in plastic wrap and refrigerate for 30 minutes.

Roll out dough: Generously flour a flat work surface. Remove one disc of dough from refrigerator. Use a rolling pin to roll dough into an 11–12-inch circle. Place rolling pin onto the dough, toward one side edge. Fold the dough onto the rolling pin, then slowly roll the rolling pin so the dough loosely wraps around it. (If the dough is stuck to the work surface, use a dough cutter to gently scrape the dough off the surface as you go.) Position the rolling pin over the pie plate, then unroll the dough into the pie plate. Press the dough into position, making sure there are no air bubbles under the dough. Repeat with the second disc of dough, leaving it on the work surface.

Make pie: Using a slotted spoon, spoon peach slices out of bowl, leaving juice in bowl. Place peach slices into bottom piecrust, distributing them evenly. Using a fork, mix cornstarch into juice left in bowl. (Juice will need to be cold for this to work, so be sure not to heat it.) Continue to mix until cornstarch is fully dissolved. Pour juice over peaches in pie. Dot peaches with butter. Working quickly, top the pie with second crust. Crimp edges and trim any excess dough. Cut 10–12 small slits in top crust. Top with coarse sugar.

Bake pie: Place in oven and bake for 10 minutes. Reduce oven temperature to 375°F. Continue to bake for 45 minutes. Remove from oven. Let cool for 4 hours. Cut and serve.

s4 e13

Tester—Jamie Francis

LEMON MERINGUE PIE

LUKE'S DINER

This is one of Rory's favorites at the diner—Luke's Lemon Meringue Pie. This recipe is made with the same tart, lemony filling you'd find in a lemon bar. If you like lemon, it'll likely become one of your favorites, too.

For crust:

1	Single 9-inch piecrust (page 189)

For lemon filling:

5	Egg yolks
1 T	Butter
¾ c	Sugar
4 T	Cornstarch
½ t	Salt
2 c	Cold water
⅔ c	Lemon juice, freshly squeezed
1 T	Lemon zest

For meringue:

5 oz	Egg whites (about 4 large eggs)
1 t	Vanilla extract
⅛ t	Cream of tartar
Pinch	Salt
10 oz	Superfine sugar (about 1½ cups)

Blind bake crust: Ensure oven rack is positioned in center of oven. Preheat oven to 325°F. Line a 9-inch pie plate with a single piecrust dough. Cover the bottom of the crust with a square of parchment paper. Then place a set of pie baking beads or 1 cup of dried beans into crust. Blind bake crust by placing it in the oven for 15 minutes. Remove and let cool.

Prepare ingredients: Place egg yolks in a medium bowl. Set aside. Place butter in a small bowl or ramekin, near stove. Set aside.

Make lemon syrup: In a medium saucepan, prior to heating, combine sugar, cornstarch, and salt. Stir to combine. Add water, lemon juice, and lemon zest. Stir until fully combined. Turn on medium heat. Using a wooden spoon or silicone spatula, stir frequently. As soon as mixture begins to boil, remove from heat.

Temper egg yolks: Begin briskly whisking egg yolks, then add 1 tablespoon of lemon syrup. Continue whisking and add 2 more tablespoons of lemon syrup. Gradually add more lemon syrup until all syrup has been added and incorporated. Return mixture to saucepan.

Thicken filling: Over medium heat, continue stirring filling. As soon as the filling starts to thicken and boil, remove from heat. Stir in butter and continue stirring for 2 minutes. Pour filling into par-baked pie shell.

Make meringue: In large mixing bowl, add egg whites, vanilla extract, cream of tartar, and salt. Beat on high speed with electric mixer until egg whites begin to form stiff peaks. Gradually add sugar. Once all sugar has been added, continue to beat on high speed for 3–5 minutes. This will help the sugar dissolve into the egg white mixture.

Add meringue: Gently scoop meringue onto lemon filling. Use a spatula to spread meringue across the entire circle, so it touches the crust around the edge of the pie. Gently dip spatula or one beater into the center of meringue, an inch or so down into it, then pull spatula straight up, while twisting, to make attractive peaks.

Bake pie: Place pie in oven and bake for 20 minutes. Remove from oven. Let cool overnight before serving. To store, leave pie sitting at room temperature. If desired, loosely tent the pie with aluminum foil.

s5 e20

Tester—Meghan Fatticci

CRÈME BRÛLÉE

SOOKIE'S KITCHEN

At the Chilton bake sale, we see Sookie surrounded by all of her magical creations. We also see her trademark klutziness in full swing, as she lights the tablecloth on fire while torching her crème brûlée.

Heed Sookie's warning—the torching step in this recipe can be dangerous. Please take precautions, and make sure your Lorelai is standing by with a few extra cups of punch.

3½ c	Heavy whipping cream
6	Egg yolks
⅔ c + ¾ c	Sugar, *divided*
¼ t	Salt
1½ t	Vanilla extract

Prepare pans and oven: Set out eight shallow 5-ounce ramekins plus two 10x14-inch glass baking dishes. Cover the bottom of each glass pan with one paper towel to provide traction for the ramekins. Place ramekins in glass dishes, making sure they all fit and are all perfectly flat. Set aside. Position two oven racks toward the center of the oven so there is space for both baking dishes, but neither rack is at the very top or the very bottom of the oven. Preheat oven to 375°F.

Make custard: In a large saucepan, bring cream to a simmer over medium heat. While cream is warming, quickly whisk the yolks in a large mixing bowl. Add ⅔ cup sugar, salt, and vanilla and whisk again until fully combined. Once cream begins to simmer, remove from heat. While quickly whisking the egg yolk mixture, pour in 1 tablespoon of the cream. Continue to whisk and add 2 tablespoons of cream. Gradually add more and more cream while continuing to whisk quickly, until all cream has been incorporated. Set aside. Set a pot or teakettle full of water to boil.

Bake custard: Ladle custard into each ramekin to just under the rim, until all ramekins are full. Open oven and pull out one rack. Carefully place one glass dish on the rack. Taking care not to get any water inside the ramekins, pour boiling water into the glass dish so it surrounds the ramekins. Water should reach halfway up the sides of the ramekins. Very gently, push the oven rack back into the oven. Repeat for the second glass dish. Bake for 15 minutes. Remove from oven and let stand for 10 minutes. Remove ramekins and refrigerate 2 hours.

Serve crème brûlées: Bring custards to room temperature. Sprinkle tops with ¾ cup sugar to form a generous layer. For the final step you'll need to use a culinary torch with great care (if you're not familiar with a culinary torch, be sure to read the instructions and practice lighting it and extinguishing it prior to torching the custards). Turn the torch on to medium-high flame. Holding the torch about 2 inches from the top of the custard, in a back-and-forth motion, begin to torch the sugar on top of each custard. This will caramelize the sugar and provide the distinctive hard shell. Continue to torch until all sugar has been torched and is a dark brown (not burned!) color. Repeat for all custards. Garnish with fresh fruit. Serve.

s1e5

Tester—Rebecca Broomall

MUD PIE
CONTRIBUTED BY HEATHER BURSON

SOOKIE'S KITCHEN

At dinner with Jackson, Lorelai, and Rune, Sookie recounts a story from back when Rory was eight years old. She and Rory had a competition to see who could make the best mud pie. Forever competitive, Sookie pulled out all the stops, not caring at all that her opponent was eight. Meanwhile, Rory made her pie out of actual mud. In the end, the two cakes looked identical.

This recipe is the Sookie version—and you'll feel like Sookie while you're making it. Bring your A game when you make this. When it's finished, you'll have a work of confectionary art so professional looking and tasting, it could win any number of competitions.

For chocolate wafer cookies:

2.5 oz	**Unsweetened baking chocolate**
1¾ c	**Flour**
½ c	**Unsweetened cocoa powder, plus extra for rolling**
¼ t	**Salt**
¼ t	**Baking soda**
½ t	**Cinnamon**
14 T	**Unsalted butter**
1 c + 2 T	**Sugar**
3 T	**Half-and-half**
1	**Egg**

For chocolate wafer cookies:

Melt chocolate: Place baking chocolate in a microwave-proof glass bowl. Place bowl in microwave. Melt chocolate in 30-second bursts set at 50 percent power. Use a wooden spoon or silicone spatula to stir in between bursts to prevent burning. Once chocolate is fully melted, remove from microwave and set aside.

Combine dry ingredients: Sift together flour, cocoa powder, salt, baking soda, and cinnamon into a medium bowl. Set aside.

Combine wet ingredients: In large bowl, using an electric hand mixer, cream together butter and sugar. Add melted chocolate and mix until incorporated. Add half-and-half and egg, beating until well mixed.

Make dough: With mixer on low speed, add dry ingredients one scoop at a time, mixing well. Dust counter with unsweetened cocoa powder. Turn dough out onto counter and knead a few times until fully incorporated.

Refrigerate dough: Divide dough in half and roll into log about 1½ inches in diameter. Wrap each log in plastic cling wrap and refrigerate 4–6 hours, or overnight, until firm.

Prepare pan and oven: Line two cookie sheets with parchment paper. Ensure oven rack is positioned in center of oven. Preheat oven to 350°F.

Slice dough: Remove one roll of dough from fridge. Work quickly before dough melts. Place plastic-wrapped dough tube on a flat surface. Roll it back and forth a few times to get a round shape. Slice dough into ⅛-inch round slices. Place dough rounds on pans about 1-inch apart. Bake for 12–14 minutes, rotating pans halfway through for even baking.

Cool cookies: Remove from oven and allow to cool on pans for 5 minutes. Place cookies on wire racks to finish cooling completely. They will crisp up as they cool. Repeat for second roll of dough.

Make 100–120 cookies.

For piecrust:

2 c	Chocolate wafer cookie crumbs
⅔ c	Chopped pecans
4 T	Butter, melted
2 T	Superfine sugar

For piecrust:

Prepare pan and oven: Line a 9-inch springform pan with parchment paper and place on cookie sheet. Set aside. Preheat oven to 350°F.

Grind cookies: Pulse a few handfuls of cookies in food processor into fine crumbs. Measure out 2 cups of crumbs. Set aside any extra crumbs and extra cookies for decorating your pie.

Mix pie dough: Return 2 cups of cookie crumbs to food processor and add chopped pecans, melted butter, and sugar, pulsing until combined.

Bake crust: Press mixture into bottom and up sides of pan, making a crust that's at least 4 inches deep. Bake at 350°F for 10 minutes. Allow to cool. Do not remove crust from pan!

Continued on the next page . . .

Eat Like a Gilmore DAILY CRAVINGS

For coffee whipped cream:

2 t	Instant coffee crystals
2 c + 2 t	Heavy whipping cream, *divided*
½ c	Powdered sugar
2 t	Heavy whipping cream
1½ t	Vanilla extract

For pie filling:

⅔ c	Heavy cream
3 c	Finely chopped high-quality, sweetened dark chocolate
16 oz	Cream cheese, softened 1
¾ c	Powdered sugar
½	Batch coffee whipped cream

For coffee whipped cream:

Combine coffee and cream: Mix coffee crystals into 2 teaspoons whipping cream until crystals are dissolved. Set aside.

Make whipped cream: Chill mixing bowl in freezer for 20 minutes. Once chilled, pour in the 2 teaspoons whipping cream plus the 2 cups. On medium-high speed, whip heavy cream into soft peaks. Slowly spoon in powdered sugar, coffee mixture, and vanilla, increasing mixer speed until stiff peaks form.

Divide and chill whipped cream: Reserve 2 cups of this coffee whipped cream for pie filling. Immediately refrigerate the rest of the whipped cream for topping your pie.

For pie filling:

Make chocolate ganache: Heat heavy cream in saucepan over medium heat until steaming, stirring constantly. Do not let simmer, boil or scorch. Remove from heat and add chocolate to hot cream, stirring gently to distribute the cream. Cover and let sit for 5 minutes to allow chocolate to soften and melt. Remove cover and stir until mixture becomes thick and creamy. This creates your ganache. Set aside ¼ cup of ganache to top your pie.

Make filling: In a separate bowl, using an electric hand mixer, cream together cream cheese and powdered sugar. Add remaining ganache and mix until combined. Reduce mixer speed to low and gently add in coffee whipped cream.

Refrigerate filling: Pour filling into crust. Cool in refrigerator 4–6 hours or overnight until firm. When cold and firm, gently remove springform pan.

Assemble mud pie: Reheat your reserved ¼ cup ganache in short bursts in microwave set on 50 percent power. Pour over top of pie, spreading to the edge of the crust. Sprinkle with chopped pecans and return to fridge until ganache is firm. Add a pile of coffee whipped cream, dust with cookie crumbs and chunks of cookies. Serve immediately and refrigerate any leftovers.

RED VELVET CAKE

WESTON'S BAKERY

When Michel suddenly starts pining for Parker, the Dragonfly's normal handyman, Lorelai cannot figure out why. Turns out, he's not really missing Parker. He's just upset he doesn't get to go to Weston's with Lorelai anymore. It used to be their special ritual—they'd make a to-do list for Parker while sharing a piece of Red Velvet Cake.

For cake:

2¼ c	Cake flour
¼ c	Cocoa powder
1 t	Baking soda
1 t	Salt
1 c	Buttermilk
3 T	White vinegar
½ c	Butter, softened
1 c	Sugar
2	Eggs
2 oz	Red food coloring

For icing:

1 c	Butter, softened
1⅓ c	Cream cheese, softened
4 t	Vanilla extract
1⅓ c	Powdered sugar

Prepare pans and oven: Cover the bottoms and sides of two 9-inch round baking pans with butter, then with a light dusting of flour. Set aside. Position oven rack in the center of oven. Preheat oven to 325°F.

Mix dry ingredients: In medium mixing bowl, combine flour, cocoa, baking soda, and salt. Lightly mix with fork. Set aside.

Prepare buttermilk: In a large glass measuring cup, combine buttermilk and white vinegar. Set aside.

Mix wet ingredients: In a large mixing bowl, using an electric hand mixer, cream together butter and sugar until smooth. Add one egg at a time, beating to mix after each.

Make cake batter: Add ⅓ of dry mixture to batter. Beat until fully blended. Add ⅓ of buttermilk, again beating until fully blended. Repeat until all dry ingredients and buttermilk have been incorporated into batter. Add red food coloring in small amounts and mix thoroughly. Continue this step until desired color is reached.

Bake cakes: Pour batter equally into each prepared pan. If possible, weigh each pan to ensure the amount of batter in each is equal. Place pans in oven at least 3 inches apart. Bake for 25–30 minutes. To test for doneness, insert a toothpick into the center of one of the cakes. If it comes out clean, the cake is done. Remove pans from oven and allow cakes to cool for 10–15 minutes.

Cool cakes: Once cakes have cooled enough that they are no longer too hot to touch, invert each pan to remove the cake layer. Wrap each layer tightly in plastic wrap. Set aside.

Make icing: In a medium mixing bowl, combine butter, cream cheese, and vanilla extract. Beat to combine. Gradually add powdered sugar, beating with mixer the whole time, until desired consistency and sweetness is reached.

Assemble cake: Unwrap each layer of cake. Place layer on a plate or cake plate. Using a spatula, spreader, or table knife, spread icing on top of the layer, about ½ inch thick. Position second layer on top. Spread icing on sides and top of cake. Serve.

Makes one 9-inch layer cake.

s6 e 14

Tester—Heather Mainz

MOCHA CRUNCH CREAM CAKE

WESTON'S BAKERY

When season 2 begins, Lorelai is engaged to Max. Like many brides, she starts leafing through bridal magazines, going on cake-tasting missions, and trying on newspaper veils. Okay, that last one may be Lorelai-specific, but you get the idea.

The cake-tasting took place at Weston's, with Lorelai in pigtails and Rory covered in guilt. Both of them knew Sookie would be making the wedding cake—so what in the world were they doing tasting cakes at Weston's?

Toward the end of the tasting, when Fran Weston announces she's going to bring out a mocha crunch cream cake, suddenly Rory's on board with the whole scheme.

Made with actual cream and chocolate-covered espresso beans, this cake may woo you over to the dark side, too.

For cake:

2¼ c	Flour
2 t	Baking powder
2 t	Baking soda
1 t	Salt
3	Eggs
1¾ c	Sugar
¼ c	Greek-style yogurt, full fat
2 T	Coffee, strongly brewed
1 T	Vanilla extract
1¼ c	Heavy cream

For icing:

½ c	Dark chocolate chips, 50–60% cacao recommended
¼ c	Semisweet chocolate chips
3 T	Butter, cubed
1¼ c	Heavy cream
2 T	Espresso powder
½ c	Powdered sugar
2 t	Vanilla extract
½–1 lb	Chocolate-covered espresso beans, *optional*

Prepare pans and oven: Cover the bottoms and sides of two 9-inch round baking pans with butter, then with a light dusting of flour. Set aside. Position oven rack in the center of oven. Preheat oven to 325°F.

Mix dry ingredients: In a medium mixing bowl, combine flour, baking powder, baking soda, and salt. Use a fork to mix the ingredients together. Set aside.

Mix wet ingredients: Crack eggs into a large mixing bowl. With an electric hand mixer on medium speed, beat the eggs. Slowly add sugar to eggs, while continuing to beat. Once fully combined, add yogurt, coffee, and vanilla. Beat until fully blended.

Make cake batter: Add ⅓ of the dry mixture to the batter and beat to mix. Next, add ⅓ of the heavy cream to batter and mix until fully combined. Repeat until all of the dry ingredients and the heavy cream have been incorporated.

Bake cake: Pour batter equally into each prepared pan. If possible, weigh each pan to ensure the amount of batter in each is equal. Place pans in oven at least 3 inches apart. Bake for 25 minutes. To test for doneness, insert a toothpick into the center of one of the cakes. If it comes out clean, the cake is done. Remove pans from oven and allow cakes to cool for 10–15 minutes.

Cool cakes: Once cakes have cooled enough that they are no longer too hot to touch, invert each pan to remove the cake layer. Wrap each layer tightly in plastic wrap. Set aside.

Mix icing: In a medium mixing bowl, add chocolates and butter. Heat heavy cream, espresso powder, powdered sugar, and vanilla extract in medium saucepan, whisking often. When mixture first begins to boil, remove from heat and immediately pour over chocolates. Let stand for 10 minutes. Stir to combine. Let icing cool.

Assemble cake: Unwrap each layer of cake. Place one layer on a plate or cake plate. Using a spatula, spreader, or table knife, spread icing on top of the layer, about ½ inch thick. Position second layer on top. Spread icing on sides and top of cake.

Add chocolate-covered espresso beans: Place beans in a large ziplock bag. Use a rolling pin to crush the beans (a hammer may be used, instead, but please lay the bag on a durable surface before using this method). Once beans are sufficiently crushed, fill your hand with crushed beans and press your palm against the side of the cake. Continue this around the entire cake, until the crushed beans are in place all around the perimeter of the cake.

Serve.

Tester—Sarah Lea Phelps

Eat Like a Gilmore DAILY CRAVINGS

CHOCOLATE RASPBERRY CUPCAKES

While Lorelai is walking and talking with Sookie, we find out Emily has ordered the chocolate raspberry cake from Weston's to serve at the party celebrating Rory's graduation from Yale. Remember—Rory first fell in love with this cake years ago when she and Lorelai were cake tasting at Weston's during Lorelai's engagement to Max. For a cake to remain a favorite for so long, its flavor must be unforgettable.

Here's your opportunity to host your own tasting. Try these cupcakes for yourself and see if you fall in love with the flavors the way Rory (and Emily) did.

For raspberry filling:

1 pt/12 oz	Raspberries, fresh, *divided* (about 2¼ cups)
¾ c	Sugar, *divided*
¾ c	Heavy cream
1 pkg	Gelatin, unflavored (¼ oz, about 1 tablespoon)
3	Egg yolks
⅔ c	Milk
½ t	Vanilla extract

For cake:

1¾ c	Flour
¾ c	Cocoa
2 t	Baking soda
1 t	Salt
¾ c	Butter
1½ c	Sugar
1 c	Greek-style yogurt, plain, full fat
3	Eggs
1 c	Coffee-flavored liqueur, Kahlúa recommended
½ c	Coffee, strongly brewed
1 t	Vanilla

For whipped cream icing:

4 c	Heavy whipping cream, cold
1 t	Cream of tartar
16 oz	Cream cheese, softened
1 c	Superfine sugar
1 t	Vanilla extract

For raspberry filling:

Prepare raspberries: Wash and dry raspberries. Set aside 1 pint of raspberries for tops of cupcakes. (Pull the prettiest, most uniformly sized and shaped berries for the toppers.) Place second pint of raspberries in medium bowl. Sprinkle with ½ cup sugar. Set aside for 1 hour. (If you are in a rush, put sugared raspberries in microwave on high for 1 minute.)

Whip heavy cream: In a cold bowl, with cold, clean beaters, whip heavy cream until it forms stiff peaks. Put in refrigerator.

Muddle raspberries: With a muddle, smash and muddle raspberries. Strain liquids into a small bowl. Scrape raspberry solids from strainer into another small bowl. Set aside.

Bloom gelatin: Sprinkle gelatin onto raspberry liquids. Set aside.

Boil water: Fill a larger saucepan, Dutch oven, or the bottom pan of a double boiler with 2–3 inches of water. Over medium heat, bring water to a boil.

Prepare remaining ingredients: Measure out remaining ingredients: 1 cup sugar, egg yolks, milk, and vanilla extract. Set aside milk and vanilla.

Whip egg yolks: Combine egg yolks and sugar in a medium mixing bowl. Mix together with a fork until a paste forms. Set aside.

Heat milk: In a medium saucepan, combine milk and vanilla extract. Over medium-high heat, bring to a boil. Remove from heat.

Temper eggs: Very slowly, begin to pour hot milk into egg yolk/sugar mixture, whisking the egg yolks. Once all of the milk has been incorporated, return mixture to saucepan or top pan of a double boiler. Stir in raspberry liquids/gelatin mixture.

Double boil custard: Place small pan containing the raspberry custard in/on the bottom pan. (The bottom of the top pan should only be touching water. Don't let it touch down all the way to the point it's touching the bottom pan.) Take care not to get any water in the custard.

Over medium-high heat, warm the custard, stirring constantly with a wooden spoon or silicone spatula. Once the custard sticks to the back of the spoon or spatula, without dripping off, it's done. Remove from heat.

Cool custard: Move custard to a medium mixing bowl. Place bowl in an ice bath or in the refrigerator. Watch custard carefully.

Make Bavarian cream: When the custard has cooled, but is still creamy (not set), remove from ice bath/refrigerator. Fold in whipped cream and raspberry solids. Cover with a sheet of plastic wrap placed directly on top of the cream. Refrigerate 30 minutes. After that, the cream will be ready to use.

For whipped cream icing:
Whip cream: (Thoroughly wash and dry beaters before completing this step. If beaters have any residue, the cream will not whip up.) In a large mixing bowl,

Tester—Heather Mainz

Eat Like a Gilmore DAILY CRAVINGS

combine heavy cream and cream of tartar. Use an electric hand mixer to begin beating the cream. Begin on a lower speed, gradually increasing speed until the mixer is running at maximum speed. With your free hand, turn the bowl, so the mixer reaches all areas. Continue to beat just until cream has formed stiff peaks. (Take care not to mix past this point, or you'll be on the road to making butter!) Stop the mixer and remove beaters from cream. Set aside.

Mix cream cheese: In a large mixing bowl, combine cream cheese, sugar, and vanilla extract. With an electric hand mixer, beat until fully combined and smooth.

Make icing: Fold the cream cheese into the whipped cream and slowly beat until blended. This is your icing.

Assemble cupcakes:
Core cupcakes: Using a cupcake coring tool or a teaspoon, core out the center of each cupcake down to the halfway point. Discard the cored pieces.

Fill cupcakes: Spoon raspberry filling into a piping bag or a one-gallon ziplock bag. Use a generous round tip (or cut a small slit in one bottom corner of the plastic bag) and pipe filling into the center of each cupcake. Bring filling up so it is flush with the top of the cupcake, or just slightly higher.

Ice cupcakes: Spoon whipped cream icing into a piping bag or a one-gallon ziplock bag. Use a generous round tip (or cut a small slit in one bottom corner of the plastic bag) and pipe icing onto the top of each cupcake. Begin by lining the outside of the cupcake, then, in one continuous motion, swirl the icing so it ends in a point in the middle. Top each cupcake with one upside-down raspberry. Serve.

Makes 30 cupcakes.

FUNNEL CAKES

FESTIVAL FOOD

Funnel cakes are a staple at Stars Hollow festivals—no matter if they take place during spring, summer, fall, or even winter.

During the Winter Festival, when Lorelai makes the offer to Luke to postpone their wedding, the funnel cake booth looms behind them as if to say, "We're still here for you, Lorelai!"

Now, funnel cakes will be there for you, too, anytime you need them.

For topping:

2 lb	Strawberries, fresh, stemmed, sliced
½ c	Sugar
2 T	Lemon juice, freshly squeezed
	Powdered sugar, for dusting
	Whipped cream, *optional*

For funnel cakes:

1½ c	Flour
¼ t	Salt
2 t	Baking powder
1	Egg
1½ c	Milk
2 T	Sugar
1 qt	Oil, for frying

Prepare strawberries: In a large bowl, combine strawberries, sugar, and lemon juice. Gently combine. Let stand at room temperature for 30 minutes.

Combine dry ingredients: In a small bowl combine flour, salt, and baking powder.

Combine wet ingredients: In a large mixing bowl, whisk together egg, milk, and sugar.

Make batter: In thirds, add dry ingredients to wet ingredients, whisking as you go.

Heat oil: Pour oil into stockpot or Dutch oven. Place a candy thermometer in pot. Over medium-high heat, heat oil to 350°F.

Prepare drying rack: Near the stove, on a flat work surface or large cutting board, stack two paper towels. Top the paper towels with a cooling rack.

Make cakes: Hold finger over bottom of funnel. Fill funnel with roughly 1 cup of batter. Place funnel over hot oil. Let batter flow from bottom of funnel in a back-and-forth pattern to make a cake. Fry cake on one side until golden brown. Flip cake and cook other side until golden brown. Use tongs to remove cake from oil and place it on drying rack. Repeat for all batter.

Serve: Place funnel cake on plate. Dust with powdered sugar. Top with strawberries and whipped cream. Serve.

Makes 6–8 5-inch funnel cakes.

s6 e 12

RECIPE GUIDE

Luke's Diner
Apple Pie, 190
Breakfast Quesadilla, 65
Cherry Danish, 17
Cherry Pie, 197
Chicken Salad, 43
Lasagna, 128
Lemon Meringue Pie, 199
Onion Rings, 95
Orange Marmalade, 25
Peach Pie, 199
Pumpkin Pie, 193
The Other Caesar Salad, 37

Sookie's Kitchen
Angel Wings with Dipping Sauce, 161
Apple Cider Ice Cream, 139
Broccoli Tarts, 11
California Roll Sushi, 105
Chocolate Biscotti, 157
Chocolate Praline Cookies, 162
Coconut Macaroons, 165
Crème Brûlée, 203
Fruit Tart, 9
Hothouse Tomato & Herb Salad, 35
Lobster Bisque, 119
Lobster Potpie, 124
Meringue Cookies, 173
Mini Orange Biscuits with Honey-Mustard
   Ham & Cheddar, 106
Mud Pie, 204

Potato Salad, 39
Soft Pretzel Goat Cheese Bites, 98
Strawberry Tarts, 6
Taquitos, 83
Valentine's Burrito, 78

Emily's Staff
Boston Cream Pie, 186
Caramelized Salmon, 121
Lobster Puffs, 88
Marzipan, 175
Passion Fruit Sorbet, 149
Sea Bass in a Lemon Dill Sauce, 123

Weston's Bakery
Apple Pandowdy, 185
Banana Cream Pie, 194
Chocolate Raspberry Cupcakes, 214
Mocha Crunch Cream Cake, 212
Red Velvet Cake, 211
Rum Balls, 159

Taylor's Soda Shoppe
Black Cow, 151
Chocolate Phosphate, 151
Egg Cream, 151
Peppermint Stick Ice Cream, 145

Town Favorite

Beef Burrito, 74
Chicken Piccata, 111
Fudge, 179
Guacamole, 71
Hard Tacos, 66
Homemade Tortillas, 73
Osso Buco, 112
Peanut Brittle, 177
Piecrust, 189
Pizza Bagels, 32
Raspberry Peach Jam, 23
Soft Tacos, 69
Sweet-and-Sour Pork, 53
Tuna Loaf, 135

Festival Food

French Dip Sliders, 97
Funnel Cakes, 219
Lemonade, 103
Roasted Turkey Legs, 115
Salty Nuts, 103

Yale Days

Chocolate Éclairs, 15
Cinnamon Buns, 12
Fried Rice, 51
Margaritas, 85
Pot Stickers, 49
Rocky Road Ice Cream, 143
Strawberry Ice Cream, 147

At Home

Biscotti, 155
Breaded French Country Chicken, 117
Caramel Apples, 181
Chocolate Chip Cookie Dough Ice Cream, 141
Fruit Turnovers, 20
Homemade Mallomars, 166
Homemade Pop-Tarts, 2
Homemade Tater Tots, 93
Mini Bagel Dogs, 90
Pizza, 29
Pizza Rolls, 31
Sugar Cookies with Icing, 170

Mrs. Kim's

Eggless Egg Salad, 41
Kimchi Dumplings, 101
Spaghetti & Wheat Balls, 126

Al's Pancake World

Egg Rolls, 46
Egg Foo Young, 55
Garlic Chicken, 57
Kung Pao Chicken, 59
Chicken in Brown Sauce, 61
Fiesta Burger, 81
Moroccan Meatball Tagine, 132

CONVERSION CHARTS

Metric and Imperial Conversions

(These conversions are rounded for convenience)

Ingredient	Cups/Tablespoons/Teaspoons	Ounces	Grams/Milliliters
Butter	1 cup/16 tablespoons/2 sticks	8 ounces	230 grams
Cheese, shredded	1 cup	4 ounces	110 grams
Cream cheese	1 tablespoon	0.5 ounce	14.5 grams
Cornstarch	1 tablespoon	0.3 ounce	8 grams
Flour, all-purpose	1 cup/1 tablespoon	4.5 ounces/0.3 ounce	125 grams/8 grams
Flour, whole wheat	1 cup	4 ounces	120 grams
Fruit, dried	1 cup	4 ounces	120 grams
Fruits or veggies, chopped	1 cup	5 to 7 ounces	145 to 200 grams
Fruits or veggies, puréed	1 cup	8.5 ounces	245 grams
Honey, maple syrup, or corn syrup	1 tablespoon	0.75 ounce	20 grams
Liquids: cream, milk, water, or juice	1 cup	8 fluid ounces	240 milliliters
Oats	1 cup	5.5 ounces	150 grams
Salt	1 teaspoon	0.2 ounce	6 grams
Spices: cinnamon, cloves, ginger, or nutmeg (ground)	1 teaspoon	0.2 ounce	5 milliliters
Sugar, brown, firmly packed	1 cup	7 ounces	200 grams
Sugar, white	1 cup/1 tablespoon	7 ounces/0.5 ounce	200 grams/12.5 grams
Vanilla extract	1 teaspoon	0.2 ounce	4 grams

Oven Temperatures

Fahrenheit	Celsius	Gas Mark
225°	110°	¼
250°	120°	½
275°	140°	1
300°	150°	2
325°	160°	3
350°	180°	4
375°	190°	5
400°	200°	6
425°	220°	7
450°	230°	8

INDEX

Beef Burrito Made with Chile Colorado, 74–77
Hard Tacos, 66–67
Moroccan Meatball Tagine, 132–133
Soft Tacos Made with Carne Asada, 69

D
dill
Eggless Egg Salad, 41
Hot House Tomato & Herb Salad, 35
Sea Bass in a Lemon Dill Sauce, 123
dumpling wrappers
Kimchi Dumplings, 101
Pot Stickers, 49

E
Egg Cream, 151
Egg Foo Young, 55
Eggless Egg Salad, 41
Egg Rolls, 46–47
egg roll wrappers
Egg Rolls, 46–47
eggs
Angel Wings with Dipping Sauce, 161
Apple Cider Ice Cream, 139
Banana Cream Pie, 194–195
Biscotti, 155
Boston Cream Pie, 186–187
Breaded French Country Chicken, 117
Breakfast Quesadilla, 65
Broccoli Tarts, 11
Cherry Danish, 17–19
Chocolate Biscotti, 157
Chocolate Chip Cookie Dough Ice Cream, 141
Chocolate Éclairs, 15–16
Chocolate Praline Cookies, 162–163
Chocolate Raspberry Cupcakes, 214–217
Cinnamon Buns, 12–13
Coconut Macaroons, 165
Crème Brûlée, 203
Egg Foo Young, 55
Egg Rolls, 46–47
Fried Rice, 51
Fruit Tart, 9

Fruit Turnovers, 20–21
Funnel Cakes, 219
Homemade Pop-Tarts, 2–5
Lemon Meringue Pie, 201
Lobster Puffs, 88–89
Marzipan, 175
Meringue Cookies, 173
Mini Bagel Dogs, 90–91
Mocha Crunch Cream Cake, 212–213
Moroccan Meatball Tagine, 132–133
Mud Pie, 204–207
Peppermint Stick Ice Cream, 145
Pizza Rolls, 31
Potato Salad, 39
Pumpkin Pie, 193
Red Velvet Cake, 211
Rocky Road Ice Cream, 143
Soft Pretzel Goat Cheese Bites, 98–99
Spaghetti & Wheat Balls, 126–127
Sugar Cookies with Icing, 170–171
Tuna Loaf, 135
endives
Other Caesar Salad, The, 37
espresso beans, chocolate-covered
Mocha Crunch Cream Cake, 212–213
espresso powder
Mocha Crunch Cream Cake, 212–213
evaporated milk, 193

F
Fiesta Burger, 81
fish
Caramelized Salmon, 121
Sea Bass in a Lemon Dill Sauce, 123
fish stock
Lobster Potpie, 124–125
French Dip Sliders, 97
Fried Rice, 51
Fruit Tart, 9
Fruit Turnovers, 20–21
Fudge, 179
Funnel Cakes, 219

G
garlic
Beef Burrito Made with Chile Colorado,

Red Velvet Cake, 211

W

Y

Z